A Real Man:

A Guide to Becoming the Men our Wives, Children and God Want Us to Be

Bruce Scifres

First published by Dog Ear Publishing
4010 W. 86th Street, Ste H
Indianapolis, IN 46268
www.dogearpublishing.net

ISBN: 978-145750-543-0

This book is printed on acid-free paper.

Printed in the United States of America

www.arealman.org

Please visit my website to receive some great ideas on how to be a better husband, father, and role model in your community. This site also has some great gift ideas for those you love. More copies of this book can be ordered from this site. Please come visit us! God Bless!

www.arealman.org

A Dedication to a Committed Warrior

David Spencer Moore graduated from Roncalli High School in Indianapolis, Indiana, in the year 2000. David was a gifted athlete and leader at our school. He was selected by his teammates as a co-captain of our 1999 undefeated state championship football team, where he was our starting defensive end. After the season, he was the proud recipient of our Leadership Award, one of the top awards given at our school. David possessed amazing physical strength. With a body weight just under two hundred pounds, he could bench-press four hundred and dead-lift six hundred pounds. To this day, he is still pound for pound the strongest student to ever walk the halls of Roncalli.

After his senior season, I created a football yearbook to commemorate our undefeated state championship campaign. I asked each of our seniors to write a short reflection on their football experience to be included in the book. David's reflection was short and quite succinct. He wrote, "The amount of success you have is dependent on the amount of faith you have. In order to achieve this faith, one must understand that no amount of iron in the weight room is equal to the iron nails of the cross." As I read his reflection, I suddenly realized the source of his strength! Certainly, God had blessed him with a strong and athletic body. His real strength, however, came from within, from what he possessed inside his heart and soul. Even as a high school student, David was unique, very mature, and wise beyond his years.

David's father, Spencer, recently retired after dedicating almost forty years to the Indianapolis Police Department. David's mother, Jo, is also a police officer, and she has been with the department for twenty-six years. As a student at Roncalli, there was never any doubt about what David would become in his adult life. Because of his work ethic, discipline, integrity, great attitude, and keen sense of honor, David was born to be a police officer. As a reflection of his wonderful parents, these qualities coursed through his veins daily.

After receiving a degree in social justice from Purdue University in 2004, David became an officer with the Indianapolis Police Department. He immediately earned the respect of his peers, and he was named Rookie of the Year in 2005. Over the next five years, he received several more commendations, including the Medal of Merit, the Medal of Honor, and the Purple Heart.

David not only gained respect and admiration from his fellow officers, he earned the same from the residents on his "beat." Though very strong and tough physically, David was friendly, kind, and had a heart filled with compassion. He got to know most of the residents on his patrol, calling many of them by name. His "families" always appreciated his diligent presence, and many thought that he was their guardian angel. Because of the intense pride he took in his work, his great personality, and his strong sense of integrity and honor, David Moore was an exceptional police officer.

At 9:01 on Sunday morning, January 23, 2011, while making a traffic stop, David was shot four times. Being a true warrior, he clung to life. God called him home three days later on January 26, 2011. The entire Indianapolis community mourned the loss of a friend, a guardian angel, and a committed community servant. Over two thousand people attended his funeral services. Beyond question, in every sense of the word, David Spencer Moore was a real man. He gave his life in service to others as a brave warrior, a true hero, and a great example for men everywhere.

Even in death, there was no part of David that was not sacrificial. He was an organ donor, and literally gave everything he had so that others might live a better life. The fortunate soul who was the recipient of his heart received a very special gift—the heart of a committed warrior. I can't think of a more valuable gift a person could receive!

David's passing occurred two weeks after I finished writing this book. As such, I am honored to dedicate this book to David and to his life well lived. David was, and will always be, a shining example of what it means to be a real man.

This prayer was written by David Moore at the end of his senior year at Roncalli High School. He delivered this prayer at the start of the All Sports Banquet for Roncalli on May 24, 2000. This prayer epitomizes how David lived his life as a high school student.

THE GREATEST COACH OF ALL

Dear Lord,

We are gathered here tonight in your name to honor those athletes who have not only taken the field for Roncalli, but who have taken to the field of battle for You.

It is not always on the sports field that we do our battle, but on the field of everyday life. We do not battle for the goals nor the touchdowns, or the blue rings, but for the cross that we will carry to You.

Allow not our memories to be filled by the highlight tapes or the dazzling plays, but instead by the prayers that began our games and the huddles we made to praise You after our victories and even our defeats.

Let us not only think it was the weight of the iron in the weight room or the long hours at practice that made us victorious, but the weight of the cross and the hours on our knees that made us great.

As for the seniors who have taken off their Roncalli jersey for the last time, help us remember that the competition has just begun. For the real battle is not with the pigskin or the round ball, but with the crosses that You have laid upon us.

Allow us to be coached by Your love, and let all of us give You, our true Coach, 110%. That is where we will find the true meaning of a champion.

In the name of Your son, Christ Jesus, we ask this blessing. Amen

OFFICER DAVID SPENCER MOORE

DATE OF BIRTH
OCTOBER 15, 1981

KILLED IN THE LINE OF DUTY
JANUARY 26, 2011

Rest in peace, David. We love you and miss you. You continue to touch our lives and inspire us still today. We know that your protective watch as a guardian angel has really just begun.

Foreword

HEADING INTO THE summer of 2009, I was asked to speak at St. Jude Parish on the south side of Indianapolis, Indiana. St. Jude is the Catholic Church across the street from Roncalli High School, where I have taught and served as the head football coach for the past twenty-one years. The two gentlemen who contacted me to give this talk asked me to speak to the men of the parish, along with any of their sons who might also attend. I was asked to address challenges that men face in today's society and to offer any suggestions that I might have in dealing with these obstacles. Since I was given a couple of months to prepare for this talk, I decided to do some research into issues that men face with balancing family life, careers, social relationships, and personal faith. Doing this research was enlightening and was very useful in helping me prepare a talk that lasted just over an hour. After the presentation, I was approached by several men who thanked me for speaking to their men's group. Many of them mentioned that they felt that more men should hear the presentation, because it contained pertinent and thought-provoking concepts.

In the months that have passed since giving this talk, I have continued to research these issues. I have become increasingly convinced that more men *do* need to be introduced to these topics in a thought-provoking way. Writing a book to explore these concepts seemed to be the best way to accomplish this task.

In my talk at St. Jude, I addressed what I called the "four cornerstones of manhood." These are the four areas of a man's life that I believe require the most time and effort for each of us to become the men we were created to be. I believe these four qualities are what truly define a "real man."
These four cornerstones are

1. being a great husband in our marriages;
2. being a strong and loving father to our children;
3. being a good role model and positive leader in our communities; and
4. striving each day to strengthen our faith relationships with God.

I have written this book with the intent of addressing each of these topics. At the end of each chapter, I conclude with an *overtime* session. In my thirty-one years as a high school football coach, I have learned that it is always wise to plan for overtime, regardless of the caliber of team we might be playing. Organizing ahead of time and practicing a clear plan of action if an overtime situation suddenly occurs can certainly make us less likely to "choke" when pressure is high and the game is on the line. Accordingly, I have concluded each chapter with an *overtime* segment to help us better prepare for the most important contest we will ever play—the game of life! I sincerely hope that the contents of this book will help you reflect on what the top priorities in your life are at this time. I would like to also add that I will devote a lot of time in this book to the topics of being a husband and father. However, I hope that any young man who is not yet married with children will still find this book interesting and worth reading. Perhaps it will provide a glimpse of married life and fatherhood for future reference.

Ultimately, I hope that it will help you take key steps toward becoming the man you want to be, as well as the man you were created to be. Let's get started, shall we?

CHAPTER 1

The Manhood Crisis

IN THE TWO hundred-plus years that America has been in existence, there has never been a greater need for the men of this country to step up and be real men. Extensive research has been done on the effects of not having the presence of strong male role models in the lives of both young males and females. The resulting statistics are both alarming and disappointing. Studies show that 82 percent of children who live with a single parent are raised by their mothers. Numerically, over eighteen million children in the United States under the age of twenty-one live with single mothers. Over one-fourth of these families live below the federal poverty level. Research also shows that the likelihood that a young man will engage in criminal activity doubles if he is raised without a father, and he likewise will be twice as likely to end up being incarcerated. The most common denominator for young men in prison is not the color of their skin, ethnic background, where they are from, or their family's financial status. The most common trait is the lack of a strong and loving father figure in their lives! Likewise, young women who grow up in the absence of a loving father figure are much more likely to seek male attention through promiscuity or other forms of misbehavior. Other statistics show that 71 percent of high school dropouts, 70 percent of juveniles in state-operated institutions, and 85 percent of all children who exhibit behavioral disorders in school come from fatherless homes. A final statistic worth noting is that 63 percent of teenage suicides are also from fatherless homes. Needless to say, young people who grow up not having a strong and loving father figure actively involved in their lives fight an uphill battle through their formative years. Oftentimes, these struggles continue well into adulthood and beyond.

What factors have led to these alarming statistics? I am certainly not an expert in this field. I do have my master's degree in education with a major in social studies, and I have been teaching and coaching for thirty-one years. As an educator, over the years, I have done a fair amount of counseling young people. Through my undergraduate and graduate coursework, I have taken classes in both psychology and sociology, and I have tried to research a great deal about these issues so that I might best be able to serve the young people I work with on a daily basis. It is with this background that I will give observations I have noticed over the years, combined with current trends in today's society.

Although children have been raised primarily by their mothers for hundreds of years, it has become more of a social issue in the past half century. Think of television programs depicting American families in the 1950s and 1960s. Most showed the husband going to work each day as his wife stayed home to take care of the kids and tend to cooking and cleaning. Although not every family operated in this fashion, it was a lot more common to have clear-cut roles for fathers and mothers in these two-parent homes. Divorce and single-parent homes were certainly less common. Since that time, there has obviously been a breakdown in family structure. We have all heard that in America today, half of all marriages that take place end in divorce. The number of unwed mothers raising children in fatherless homes has also increased substantially. Although the reasons for these new family dynamics are too numerous to address in this chapter, the one factor I would like to focus on centers around men who have priorities in the wrong places. In this chapter, I would like for us to address issues that we as men have some control over. Let us focus on ourselves first before we worry about others.

Being a man in today's world is not easy. Growing up, we are bombarded by conflicting messages. Whether it is advertising, TV programs, movies, or the Internet, many of these messages are misleading as to what it means to be a real man. So many forms of media insinuate that in order to be successful, you must have a high-paying job so that you can afford nice clothes, a nice car, a huge home, and have plenty of social opportunities. Oftentimes, the means by which this wealth is achieved in much of the media we observe might be dishonest or illegal. Being misguided by this same media and today's society, many teenage boys also equate masculinity and manhood to sexual conquests. Again, much of what they see in the various forms of media tends to validate this notion. Consequently, many young men have a very distorted view of how to treat young women, and they fail to appreciate females and their true worth as creations of God. The notion that it is OK to cheat or lie to get what you want or to get ahead of the next guy is prevalent. For many young men, integrity and good character are sorely lacking. As these young men become young adults, it is no wonder that so many are willing to mistreat the women in their lives and shirk the responsibilities of fatherhood when they arrive at that point in their lives. It is so much easier and more convenient to continue on with their self-centered ways than to accept responsibility for their actions and do what is right.

Now, certainly young men are not always the only ones who need to accept blame. Many young ladies do not have their priorities straight, either, and they can be just as prone to making bad decisions and can be just as selfish. But as was mentioned in the first paragraph of this chapter, 82 percent of children who live with a single parent live with their mothers. This is why I am going to spend the rest of this chapter focusing on the man's role in this equation.

Although there is not one clear-cut solution that can solve all of the problems mentioned at the start of this chapter, I believe that many of these issues could be solved if men would commit to prioritizing their vocations as men over their occupations as men. Let's begin to explore the difference between these concepts.

A man's occupation is what he does to generate income to provide for his family. Certainly, maintaining a job and providing food, clothing, and shelter for one's family is vitally important and would certainly be included on a job description for any father and husband. However, I will contend that a real man's vocation is more important than his occupation. *Webster's Dictionary* defines vocation as "The function or career toward which one believes oneself to be called." In other words, our vocations are what we are "called" to do in this life. For a married man with children, his calling should be first and foremost his family—and what is best for his wife and kids. This is where potential conflict lies.

I am a firm believer that what a man does from nine to five in his occupation should simply be the means by which he supports his *vocation* as a husband and father. Doing what is best for his family should be his real "calling" in life. I realize that many people feel that they are answering a "calling" in their careers, especially if they are involved in doing something where they are serving others. As a high school teacher and coach, I do feel that I am called to help others. I think most educators feel this way. Likewise, I'm sure most nurses, doctors, law enforcement officers, firefighters, and so forth feel that they are being called to serve others. Feeling this way about our careers typically leads to great job satisfaction. However, I do believe our roles as husbands and fathers are more of a true *vocation* and "calling" in regard to where our priorities should lie. The ongoing struggle that many men face is that, in our desire to get ahead career-wise so that we can provide nicer things for our loved ones, quality time with family is often sacrificed in the process. Studies show that most children, if given a choice, will almost always choose spending *time* with their fathers over toys or gifts. Children definitely need and crave quality time with *both* parents. Likewise, most wives want and need quality time with their husbands. It is important for a man to dedicate time to listening and communicating with his wife on a frequent basis, or she will begin to feel detached and neglected in the relationship. We will talk in more detail about this in the next chapter. Suffice it to say that if a man wants to be a vital part of the lives of his wife and children, he must be willing to commit quality time to both.

The key to maintaining healthy relationships within our families is creating a balance with our time and setting priorities. This sounds so simple but can oftentimes prove to be problematic. If we truly begin to develop the attitude that our careers are really just the means of supporting our *vocations* as husbands and fathers, prioritizing our time becomes easier to accomplish. As we pull ourselves away from work to try to get home at a more reasonable hour, we then must ask ourselves, "How can I best spend quality time with my family?" If we use this extra time to go golfing with our buddies, or if we confine ourselves to the home office and bury our noses in the newspaper or become glued to the TV, we really are not fulfilling our *vocations* as family men. Although we are away from work at the office, we still are not really available for our wife and kids! Remember, what our children—and usually our wives—want is our undivided attention. They deserve no less!

Overtime

We have just explored the immense problems caused by the lack of a strong and loving father figure in the lives of young people. Collectively, men need to do a better job of stepping up and accepting our roles as fathers and husbands and the responsibilities that go with these positions. In short, we need to embrace our vocations as husbands and fathers. Mark Twain once said, "The secret of success is to make your vocation your vacation." In other words, as husbands and fathers, we need to view our wives and children as real blessings in our lives, and strive to have fun and gain much joy and happiness in our daily interactions with them. As more men accept and take on these challenges, many of the societal woes we discussed at the beginning of this chapter will begin to decline. A real man should be willing to do what needs to be done to meet these challenges!

In the next chapter, we will address more specifically the issues we face in trying to be good husbands to our wives. As we discuss these challenges, we will also share some ideas on how to become the men our wives want us to be. I know that sounds a little scary, but I am confident that as we delve into the qualities of a real man, we will see that the things our wives want most from us are pretty much the same as what our children and God want from us—and that can't be that bad! Let's continue on this journey toward manhood!

CHAPTER 2

"Wherefore Art Thou, Romeo?"

IN THIS CHAPTER, we are going to focus on the first cornerstone of manhood. This relates to men being great husbands for their wives. Before we can discuss different ways to be better husbands, we need to first acknowledge that there are certainly fundamental differences between men and women. These differences are oftentimes just as profound mentally and emotionally as they are physically. As humans, researchers say that most of us have four basic emotional needs, which are

1. the need to love and to be loved;
2. the need to belong;
3. the need for a good self-image; and
4. the need for autonomy or to be able to function independently without control by others.

These basic emotional needs are shared by both men and women. As we grow and mature, if any of these four components are missing or are not properly developed, there will probably be issues that will need to be resolved in our adult lives. Likewise, these emotional needs do not disappear as we become adults.

Sometimes they become even more profound as we age. As husbands, we need to be mindful of these basic needs, both for our own sakes and the happiness of our spouses. Throughout this chapter, I will periodically refer back to these fundamental needs.

As we have listed some similarities between most men and women, let's now look at some primary differences. I want to start by saying that these traits are generalizations that apply to most men and women, but they are certainly not always true. Depending on upbringing and environmental background, some people might vary widely from these tendencies. However, these are good "rule of thumb" guidelines. Having a basic knowledge of these tendencies can certainly be helpful in enriching and nourishing a marriage relationship.

Let's begin with physiological differences in the brains of boys and girls. Girls tend to develop the right side of their brains faster than boys develop theirs. This leads to better language skills, such as talking, pronunciation, vocabulary, and earlier reading. Girls usually grow up being better able to express themselves. In regard to environmental influences, researchers say that mothers tend to talk to, look at, and make more eye contact with their infant daughters than they do with sons. Girls are oftentimes caressed and stroked more than boys. This may be why girls tend to be more social and better able to interpret emotions than boys. As teenagers, girls tend to talk about other people, and they strengthen friendships by sharing secrets, hopes, and dreams with their close friends.

Conversely, boys tend to develop the left side of their brains faster than girls develop theirs. Consequently, boys usually have better visual-spatial skills and perceptual skills. Boys are usually better at problem solving, math, building, solving puzzles, and are drawn toward manipulating things with their hands. Young boys tend to be handled more physically, with more roughhousing, and tend to respond by being more physical and aggressive as they play. Both males and females have testosterone in their bodies, but the higher amounts in a boy's system also leads to being more physical by nature. While teenage girls tend to talk mostly about people, teenage boys usually talk about sports and objects or things and how they work. For most teenage girls, the biggest event in life is to have a boyfriend. Teenage boys tend to be most interested in sports, video games, and cars. They might talk about sex, but they don't usually talk much about girlfriends or relationships. Not surprisingly, these same tendencies carry over into adulthood. Most women talk about relationships, people, clothing, their weight, and physical appearance. Men tend to talk about sports, work, news, politics, cars, and how things work. Keeping with these themes, at family functions or social gatherings, women tend to sit in groups and discuss people and relationships, while most men prefer to be doing something like shooting hoops, throwing a ball, and so on as they talk mainly about things and not so much about people, relationships, or feelings.

Men and women also gain self-esteem in different ways. A man's sense of self is usually defined through success in achieving results and accomplishments. These accomplishments are many times career related, and they create the most pride if the man achieves these goals by himself. Most men are motivated when they feel needed. Women experience sense of self through their feelings and the quality of their relationships. Women value love, personal connections, relating, and communication. Females are motivated when they feel special or cherished.

Women are also very concerned with physical attractiveness. Men might also show concern for their appearance, but to a different degree. Gentlemen, here is food for thought—how many more pairs of shoes does your wife own than you? How much longer does it take your wife to get ready to go out than it does you? Who is more inclined to try on several outfits before choosing what to wear? Who spends more time in front of a mirror when getting ready? When you and your wife are packing clothes to go on vacation, who takes the longest, and who packs more? The answers to all of these questions are probably pretty obvious, and all of them point to one thing. How our wives think they look, and even more importantly, how they feel *we* think they look is extremely important to them! The first three of the four basic emotional needs listed at the start of this chapter (the need to love and to be loved, the need to belong, and the need for a good self-image) are especially strong for our wives. Now combine this knowledge with the understanding that women place a high value on communication, relating, and sharing thoughts and feelings. There is an old saying that the way to a man's heart is through his stomach. The way to a woman's heart is a little more complex, but having an understanding of the concepts we have just discussed should help us head in the right direction.

Let's summarize this information into a list of things that most women want and need from their husbands, as well as ways we husbands can accomplish what they need.

1. Affirm them daily. Every wife wants to know that she is loved and that she is still her husband's sweetheart. Make a point of telling her daily that you love her! Holding her hand when you walk and an unexpected hug or kiss are also great ways to say, "I love you!"
2. Let them know that they are still beautiful. Tell them so frequently! Being good and sincere about complimenting their appearance and what they do well will make their hearts happy and boost their confidence and self-image!
3. Be a good communicator with daily conversation. Remember how important this is for females. Make time each day to talk and especially to listen as she shares her thoughts.
4. Make quality time with wives and children a priority. Our wives desperately want us to be good fathers to our children.
5. Be understanding and show forgiveness when our wives make mistakes. They are human. The better job we do with this, the more they will forgive us when we say or do something dumb (which we men are all prone to do. It's in our DNA!).

6. Show kindness and affection daily. Sometimes married couples forget or just take this for granted.

7. Share household and child-rearing responsibilities. I have read before that many women find their husbands to be most attractive when they are cleaning, vacuuming, or playing with the kids. Being attractive to our wives can certainly have its rewards!

8. Take care of our own health and well-being. Our wives and children need us to be there for them. Better health means a higher quality of life and more enjoyment for everyone in the family.

9. Become the spiritual leader in the household. Oftentimes it is the mother who gets the kids ready for church and initiates spirituality in the home. I think most women would love to see their husbands take the lead in this department. In doing so, we set a great example for our children as we prepare them not only for the rest of their lives, but for eternity. I hope we all feel that our children need and deserve this!

These nine suggestions are all ways that we can show our wives that they are a priority in our lives and that we care about them and want them to be happy. Following these guidelines can certainly create stronger bonds in our relationships and ultimately strengthen our marriages. Does working each day to become a better husband mean that we become less manly or masculine? Does it mean that when we are with our male friends we need to all sit in a circle and share our deepest feelings as we pass around a box of tissues? The answer to both these questions is an obvious no! When we are with our male friends, we can still do what males do and just be one of the guys. However, we can at the same time be good husbands who have strong connections with our wives without losing our masculinity.

My wife Jackie and I have been married now for twenty-four years. I can honestly say that I have *always* felt blessed to be her husband. I can also say, without question, that I love her more today than I did when we were first married. My love for her has grown, because I now better understand and appreciate the fine person she chooses to be. She has always been a positive influence on me, and she inspires me to want to be a better man. My faith in God has grown stronger because of our relationship, and we are both committed to raising our four children in a Christian home. We both firmly believe that our children are our most precious gifts from God, and as such, we feel it is our duty to lead them on their journey back to God. I am honored to share this task with my wife!

Jackie and I are proud to say that we have a good and happy marriage. Certainly, I am not the perfect husband (Jackie could easily validate this point). But I do know that she appreciates my efforts to try to follow the nine guidelines we discussed earlier. I feel she deserves a good husband and a happy marriage. She has faithfully loved me, in spite of my shortcomings, and she has been a loyal friend. Even though she comes across as somewhat shy and quiet to those who don't know her well, she is witty and has a great sense of humor. She has always been able to really make me laugh! Being around her makes me happy. Although we have both entered middle age and Mother Nature and gravity have both begun to work their evil magic to change our youthful looks, she is still beautiful to me. Knowing that she has faithfully loved me all of these years and is such a wonderful mother to our children makes her all the more attractive. Sometimes she will catch me looking at her and will wonder if something is wrong. The truth is that she really is beautiful to me! I make a strong effort to tell her frequently that she looks pretty or that she looks cute in her outfit or that I think she is beautiful. I make sure that I tell her daily that I love her. I also try to tell her these things in front of our children. Seeing her smiling and happy brings joy to my heart. I do feel both lucky and blessed to be her husband. Being unfaithful to Jackie has never been an option for me, because I refuse to let it be. As I see it, twenty-four years ago, we stood in a church in front of all of those we loved the most—our families, our best friends, and God. We promised each other, and all those in attendance, that we would love, cherish, and honor each other until parted by death. We deliberately chose those words and made that promise before God. I think she and I both feel honor-bound to carry out these vows. Although any marriage can be challenging at times, ours has been fulfilling and full of much love and joy.

I believe that strong communication is at the core of any good relationship. Jackie and I have always talked very easily, and I try to allow some time each day for us to just sit and chat. We have always been good about talking and sharing. After she and I had been married for about a year, we went on a hayride with about twenty other couples. The hosts of the party had us all play a game where we had to answer about twenty questions about our spouse. The questions were mostly random, such as questions about shoe size, favorite color, favorite food, favorite movie, and so on. The couple who had the greatest number of correct answers about each other won a small prize. Jackie and I won handily, even though many of the other couples had been married much longer than we had. She and I have always talked and shared quite well. I believe that communication is the key to bonding and creating connections in a relationship. Because of this connection, I now realize that after all of these years, I not only still love my wife, but I am still very much *in love* with my wife. It brings me much happiness to know that Jackie feels the same way!

About a year ago, I ran an idea past the other married coaches on our football staff. They all thought it was a good idea. We all invited our wives to go to a Saturday night Mass together, with the understanding that we would all go to dinner afterward. Our wives didn't know, however, what we had planned immediately after Mass. I stopped and picked up a dozen roses beforehand and secretly hid them in the church. I had made arrangements with the priest, Father Jim Wilmoth, to stay after Mass. We waited until everyone had left the church, under the guise that we were "visiting" before going to dinner. Father Wilmoth, who is a wonderful man and an amazing priest, asked us to all have a seat. Our wives did not have a clue that this was going to happen. He began to speak about the beauty and sanctity of marriage and the qualities that create lasting love. When he was finished, I grabbed a rose, stood in front of the group, and began speaking to Jackie. I first thanked her for being my loving wife and for all of the sacrifices she had made over the years to allow me to teach and coach at a school like Roncalli. I then told her how much I respected and admired her for the person she chooses to be and that being married to her has made me become a better man. I thanked her for being such a wonderful mother to our children and for being such a positive influence in making our house a loving home. I told her that she is more beautiful to me now than the day we met. Finally, I shared that I am more in love with her now than ever before, that I am proud to be her husband, and that I look forward to spending the rest of my life with her! I then handed her the rose, gave her a hug and a kiss, and sat down next to her. Each of our assistant coaches, one by one, addressed their wives in similar fashion in front of the group. It was awesome to see our "rough-and-tough" football coaches share their love and devotion to their wives in one another's presence. When the last coach had finished, we all stood together. Father Wilmoth then led each couple, one by one, as we renewed our wedding vows. As was promised, we then all went out to dinner together.

I was happy that we were able to do this as a coaching staff for our wives. The life of a coach's wife is often a challenging and thankless job. I think our wives were surprised and genuinely thankful for our creative way of expressing our love and appreciation for them. With some effort and commitment, combined with a better understanding of the similarities and differences between men and women, hopefully we can all improve our marriage relationships. With some effort, we can all take steps toward becoming the men our wives want us to be!

Overtime

We focused in this chapter on making an effort to become better husbands for our wives. Likewise, a real man should always strive to be a good son to his mother and father. My mom is now eighty-nine years old, and my dad is eighty-seven. I feel so blessed to still have them both as such a vital part of my life and the lives of my children. They recently celebrated their sixty-seventh wedding anniversary. They have been such great examples of commitment, sacrifice, and enduring love for their children and all who know them. My mother is one of the most unselfish people I have ever known. She has sacrificed and given everything she has to try to make sure that her eight children have everything we need. She is also one of the strongest people I know. Over the years, she has fought through a near-fatal car accident, joint replacement, severe arthritis, and breast cancer. Through it all, I have rarely ever heard her complain, since she would never want to burden her children with her problems. As we were growing up, she was our primary teacher in matters relating to God and the church. Every Sunday, she made sure that all eight of us were fed, dressed, and loaded up to head to Sunday school and the weekly church service. It was through this determined introduction to God, and through watching my mother do her best to raise eight children, that I began to understand the attributes of unconditional love. Even at eighty-nine years of age, she still ranks right there with my wife and two daughters as one of the four most beautiful women I have ever known.

Each year, on February 14, I drop off a card—sometimes in her mailbox or perhaps on her front door. It's usually a silly, homemade card asking her to be my valentine. Knowing her, she wouldn't want anything too plush or expensive. Yet, I want her to know how much I love her and that she will forever hold a special place in my heart. Every time I see her, I make sure to tell her that I love her and that she looks beautiful to me. She deserves that!

Likewise, my father was a very hard worker and a great role model. His father died when my father was thirteen years old—in the middle of the Great Depression. As a result, my father lived a rather hard childhood and actually had to leave his mother for a while to live in an orphanage. He did not finish high school, as he joined the navy during World War II. As a young man, he became a welder and continued that career until his retirement. Being a caring father and provider, he tried to work as much overtime as possible. Throughout my childhood, most days, I recall him coming home late, dirty, and exhausted. While I was growing up, my dad wasn't overly expressive with words of love, yet we all knew that he loved us deeply. As he has gotten older, it has become much easier for him to express his love for his children and grandchildren. Every time I see him now, we hug and tell each other "I love you." I think he needs and appreciates this as much as I do.

Dad has taught me many things over the years—to work hard, to be humble, to be thankful for what I have, and, above all else, to love God. The most valuable and cherished lesson, however, has come from witnessing my parents' sixty-seven years of marriage. During that span, there have certainly been troubled times, but they have always stuck to the vows they made before God so many years ago. I have heard that the best way a father can show his children that he loves them is to show his children that he loves their mother. For the past six or seven years, my mother has struggled to get around and has had to rely on using a walker. Dad has been a wonderful caregiver during this time. Watching my father's devotion to her as he works so hard to keep her comfortable has made me prouder than ever to be his son. I can't imagine a better example of what it means to be a real man. Now more than ever, I hope that someday I can grow up to be like him.

Not long ago, my parents were telling me that they were very proud of me for the things I have accomplished and especially proud of the man I have become. I told them that anything good that I have accomplished in this life is a reflection of them and my upbringing. I want them to know how much I've appreciated their unconditional love over the years, how much I love them in return, and how proud I am to be their son. Likewise, I hope my own children can see each day how much I love and respect their mother, and through observing my devotion to her, I hope they gain a better understanding of how much I love them. These two are certainly interconnected, and that leads us into the next chapter and a look at the second cornerstone of manhood.

CHAPTER 3

The Gift Of Fatherhood

THE STORY IS told that one night, a father overheard his son pray: "Dear God, make me the kind of man my daddy is." Later that night, the father got on his knees and prayed, "Dear God, make me the kind of man my son wants me to be." I have no doubt that both the father and his son in this short story went on to have very happy lives based on a wonderful father-son relationship.

In the foreword, I mentioned that the second cornerstone of manhood is being a strong and loving father for our children. In chapter 1, I spoke of our vocations, or callings, as husbands and fathers. Let's put these two together and explore in more detail this wonderful gift of fatherhood.

I first began to understand this concept of our children being *gifts* as I was in the delivery room with Jackie as each of our four children came into this world. Anyone who has ever witnessed the miracle of childbirth should have an understanding of the power of this life-changing event. As a person of faith, one can't help but feel the presence of God as our child first arrives, lets out that first blood-curdling scream, and then takes in those first few breaths of air. As we hold our newborn for the first time, look at those tiny feet, hands, and precious little face, knowing that this bundle of joy was conceived with the one we love, having a sense of divine involvement is inevitable. I have always felt that our four children were specifically selected for Jackie and me as precious gifts from God. I felt that way on the day they were born, and I continue to feel that way as they are now all in their teenage years edging toward independence. I have no doubt that I will always feel this way, regardless of their ages or where life might lead them. I do believe that our children are gifts that God has given us on loan. I also believe that our existence here on earth is simply part of our journey back to God. Our time on earth will eventually come to an end; it is inevitable. Hence, I believe that it is our duty as parents to help guide our children on their life journeys back to God and his kingdom. I also believe that one day we will be held accountable for how well we handle this assignment.

I have grown to believe that my first job as a father is to strive each day to convince my children that I love them. Victor Hugo, the famous French poet said, "Life's greatest happiness is to be convinced that we are loved." I think this is especially true when we are dealing with our children. I truly believe that this is imperative to their development and sense of well-being. In an effort to convince my children of this each day, I try to tell them daily that I love them. Ever since they were little, the last thing I tell them before they go to bed is "Remember to dream tonight about how much your dad loves you." Before they started high school, my job each morning was to wake up each of our four children to start the day. To keep them from waking up grouchy, I rubbed each of their backs for three or four minutes. I also used this time to reinforce what I had told them the night before. About fifteen seconds into their backrubs, I would pause and ask, "Did you remember to dream last night about how much your dad loves you?" They all knew they had to give me an affirmative answer before their back rub would continue. This form of bribery each morning made them verbally acknowledge that they knew their dad loved them. It also allowed me to reinforce this message to start and end each day. As they are older now, and they all seem to get up at different times, I seldom go through this morning wake-up routine. However, I still tell them each night as they are going to bed to remember to dream about how much their dad loves them. I also try to tell them at other times each day that I love them, especially when I am leaving the house. If, by chance, something were to happen and God decided that it was time for me to leave this earth, I do not want there to be any doubt whatsoever about whether their father loved them. This is extremely important to me.

Even more than the verbal communication, I hope my actions each day convince them that they are loved. I think one of the greatest gifts we can give our children is to let them know that we believe in them. This can be accomplished by showing our appreciation for them by being patient, kind, and forgiving. We only have a limited time to make a lifelong impression on our children. By making the effort to spend quality time with our kids, we validate that they are important and a priority in our lives. Whether this time is spent reading to them, playing games, helping them with homework, or just sitting and asking them about how their days have gone, we are showing them that we are interested and that we believe they are worthwhile. It is important that our children know that they are loved unconditionally by their parents and that they can count on us being there for them. As fathers, we need to be generous with affection as we cuddle, hug, and kiss them daily. Studies show that children need affection from both parents for healthy development. As the primary male role model in their lives, we should certainly not be stingy in this department!

Along with convincing our children that we love them, we must also strive to be the type of person we want our children to be. The best way we can teach this is by being a great role model. I think every parent wants his or her child to grow up to be a hard worker and to possess honesty, integrity, kindness, discipline, gratitude, and honor. Guess what, guys? We, along with their mothers, are the primary teachers of these traits and have more of an influence on their lives in this regard than anyone else. If we want our children to become adults with character and become good citizens, we must model these traits in our daily lives. On the day our child is born, we are not handed a manual with all of the right answers on how to raise kids. However, common sense tells us that the best way to give guidance on how to be a good person is to live our lives accordingly. Probably more than we want to admit, their eyes are upon us, watching and learning life lessons by our daily conduct. Good or bad, odds are that our children will imitate what they have observed from us as they become adults. This is an awesome responsibility, and at the same time, it is a wonderful opportunity for us to help our children become the people God created them to be. The good news is that we don't have to run the forty-yard dash in 4.5 seconds, bench-press three hundred pounds, look like Brad Pitt, be a genius, or make a six-figure income to be real men. To be great dads, we don't need to be perfect, but we do need to be present in their lives.

In the *overtime* segment of chapter 2, I wrote that perhaps the best way a father can show his children that he loves them is to show his children that he loves their mother. In so many ways, I do believe this to be true. One of the primary needs our children have, along with the need to feel loved, is to feel security in their lives. A strong, loving relationship between their parents is the first place they receive this security. The example set by the father in a marriage relationship is crucial. A son will always look to his father for direction and guidance. If he sees his father as a man of strength and character treating his mother with love, devotion, honor, and respect, he will treat his mother the same way. Just as importantly, he will grow into an honorable man of strength and character and will treat his future wife with that same love, devotion, honor, and respect. This becomes perpetual, as his sons and grandsons will learn these same life lessons about how to be a real man.

Likewise, the way a father treats his wife will have a profound affect on his daughter. If a father treats his wife with love, kindness, devotion, and respect, his daughter will learn how she should expect to be treated and how to choose the men in her life.

Daughters tend to choose men based on how their fathers treat women. A good rule of thumb, gentlemen, is to always treat our wives the way we want our daughters to be treated by their future husbands. More times than not, this will become a self-fulfilling prophesy. As fathers, it is imperative that our daughters know that we love and cherish them as special gifts from God. A big part of a young lady's self-esteem is based on her relationship with her father. If she does not receive love, support, and affection from her dad, she will seek it from other males elsewhere! Studies show that weak father-daughter relationships often lead to a higher inclination toward promiscuity. The multitude of societal problems we mentioned in chapter 1 that occur from fatherless homes apply just as much with young ladies as it does with young men.

I am the very proud father of four teenage children. The second and fourth children are girls. As I am writing this book, Abby is seventeen and a junior at Roncalli High School where I teach and coach. Meggie, our youngest, is thirteen and a seventh grader at Nativity, a nearby Catholic grade school. It is hard to believe that she is just a couple of years away from being at Roncalli. Abby and Meggie are both beautiful young ladies. Thank goodness they got their looks from their mother! Like most fathers of beautiful teenage daughters (and I hope every father believes from the bottom of his heart that his daughters are beautiful), this dating thing has me a bit concerned.

Two years ago, as Abby was getting ready to come into Roncalli as a freshman, I decided to lay the groundwork for what my expectations were if any of our football players thought about asking her out. Again, she is a very pretty young lady! At our preseason rules meeting, I stood in front of our 150 players, freshman through seniors, and delivered this speech: "Gentlemen, for the first time since I have been coaching at this school, I am going to have a daughter at Roncalli. Now, I realize there will come a time when she will begin dating. Since I know most of you pretty well and believe you to be men of character, when she does start dating, I would just as soon have her date a football player. However, as her father, I do have some rules for dating my daughter that I want you all to be very aware of. Since the day she was born, I have loved her more deeply than you can imagine, at least until you have a daughter of your own. Because of this, if you take her out, these are my four rules, and they will be followed:

Rule #1: Treat her with respect. If you make her cry, I will make you cry!

Rule #2: I realize that it is fashionable for some young men today to be sporting the "sag" look where your pants are hanging down showing off your underwear. If you show up at our house and give me any indication whatsoever that you don't know how to keep your pants pulled up properly, I will take care of that situation immediately—with my staple gun.

Rule #3: If you are in the presence of me or my wife, do not put your hands on my daughter. If you do, I will first physically remove your hands from my daughter's body, and then I will physically remove your hands from your body—with a hatchet.

Rule #4: If you take my daughter out, there *will* be a curfew. If you do not have her home when she is supposed to be home, I will go on a hunting expedition. Just like any good safari, the hunt will end with a head mounted to a plaque in my office. A real creative mind is not necessary to figure out whose head will be mounted on my wall!"

I went through this speech in front of 150 teenage boys without cracking a smile. Because of the bond and relationship coaches develop with their players, I felt comfortable giving this address. Our older players knew me well enough to understand my sense of humor, so they chuckled and got a kick out of it. However, most of the freshmen listened intently with their eyes and mouths wide open. I could almost see the wheels spinning inside their adolescent minds as they were thinking, "Is this guy nuts?" I think there is probably a lot of merit to teenage boys thinking that the father of the girl they are asking out might be half crazy. I think I will keep it that way.

In spite of the fact that my teenage daughter heard about this speech and was convinced that I had ruined her social life forever and that she would *never* go out on a date, she has been asked out by more than one young man, and she did have a date for this year's homecoming dance and also a date for the prom. As I explained to her later, I expect any young man that asks her out to treat her with the utmost respect. I refuse to accept anything less. Likewise, I want her to accept nothing less!

As a young man, I used to vow that I would never let a young lady wrap me around her little finger. I just never thought this would be to my best interest. Yet, Jackie says I am oblivious to the spell my daughters have cast upon me. Every time I see Abby or Meggie smile, my heart melts. I enjoy so much being able to lightheartedly tease them and watch them interact with each other, their brothers, and Jackie. There is never a day that goes by that they don't make me smile. Ever since all four of our kids were little, Jackie and I would flash three fingers at them symbolizing "I love you." We use different fingers for each of them to make it unique. I have had Abby in class a couple of times since she has been at Roncalli. Periodically, in class when no one else is looking, I will flash her the "three" sign. At first, I think she was terrified that someone might see her old, fat dad flashing finger signals to her. Sometimes, when she glances up, I will "scratch" my head with three fingers. This generally makes her smile. I simply want her to know that no matter where we are, I love her very much and am so proud to be her dad. She is more relaxed now, and as we pass each other in the halls, we simply say, "Three."

Likewise, I try to remind Meggie daily that I love her. As a thirteen-year-old, when she sees me coming, she will oftentimes run.

I have to chase her around the house and catch her before I can kiss her cheek. The harder I have to work to catch her, the more smooches her cheek receives. Although she struggles with me a bit, she is always giggling. I really don't think she minds it that much when I catch her and the face smooches commence. Most nights when I get home from work and see Abby or Meggie, I will bellow, "Hey, there is Miss *Bee-Yoo-Tee-Full!*" in a loud and exaggerated voice. They both act like they think their dad is the world's biggest goof. That's OK; I'm perfectly fine with that as long as they know that I love them! My two daughters have brought so much love and joy to my heart. I know that they have touched my life in a way that only daughters can. Moreover, I know that my life will never be the same because of it. I can only pray that they receive the same amount of love and joy from me.

Like most men who want to have children, I had always dreamed of having sons of my own. As a father, I want my sons to grow to become strong, hardworking, humble, respectful, kind, loving, devoted, honorable men of character. Over the years, I have honestly tried to model these traits for my sons. They say that you often will not see the fruits of your labor as a parent until your children are grown and out on their own. I feel blessed, because I've already begun to see the type of man our oldest is becoming. Luke is now nineteen years old. He graduated in the spring of 2010 from Roncalli. From the day he was born, I had dreamed of having the opportunity to coach him at Roncalli. As a senior player for us last year, he proved to be a unique young man. Toward the end of his junior year, he wrote a grant proposal to the United Way and received a $2,300 grant to start an Athletes Against Drug and Alcohol Abuse (AADAA) program at Roncalli. By organizing several fun events at our school, he led over two hundred of our students to sign pledge cards promising not to use drugs or alcohol during their time at Roncalli. As he founded this organization, he knew that this would not be considered "cool" by some of the student body. He also knew that some of his teammates, after they had played their last game and no longer had the threat of athletic suspension hanging over their heads, would turn to partying in their senior year. Finally, he knew that if he were to stand by his pledge, he would not be able to go to Florida over spring break his senior year with the large group of his classmates who were going. He held true to his promise, and he told me later that there was no way he would allow himself to be in a position where he might get in trouble and cause embarrassment to me—his father and head football coach. Because of his character, integrity, and strong convictions, I don't think that he would have been selected on any "Most Popular" lists for his class. Yet, he always seemed to be okay with that, knowing that he was doing the right thing and striving each day to make his dad proud. He had a very good senior football season as our starting slotback. He averaged right at seven yards per attempt each time he carried the ball and became one of the better edge-blocking backs we have had in a while. Far beyond his accomplishments on the field, however, I was most proud of how he represented himself in the hallways at school and as a member of the team. It is customary for our sophomores to stay after practice each day and carry all of the equipment back to the barn. As a senior, Luke stayed after each day to help the sophomores carry equipment. This was the first time a senior had ever done this. He also anonymously wrote letters to all 114 varsity players (sophomores through seniors) explaining what he admired most about each of them, and he included the Bible verse from Phil. 4:13; "I can do all things through Christ who strengthens me" typed at the bottom of each letter. Many of the players asked if the coaches were writing these, saying that they were inspirational. Many of them taped these letters to the inside of their lockers. Luke also sent one of these letters to each of our ten varsity coaches. I was the only one who knew where the letters were coming from. He anonymously placed these letters in each player's locker throughout the season, not expecting recognition or anything in return. He said that he hoped it would promote good team chemistry if nobody knew where they were coming from. After his senior season, his hard work, character, and integrity paid off. He was selected as the recipient of the Indianapolis Kiwanis Club Mental Attitude Award. All twenty-eight high schools in the Indianapolis area nominate players for this top award, and he became the first player from Roncalli to be the overall winner. At the end of his senior year at Roncalli, the school's athletic department selected him as the male Mental Attitude Award winner for the school year. He was also chosen as the recipient of the Robert F. Tully scholarship. This award is named in honor of a long-time and much beloved teacher and coach at Roncalli. It is based on acts of Christian love and self-giving consistent with the life and work of Mr. Bob Tully. I was so proud that he received each of these awards, primarily because he had worked so hard to make good decisions and to do the right thing, even when so many others were choosing to take the more popular route. Luke is now a freshman and playing football at Marian University in Indianapolis. Marian is a wonderful school, and their team made it to the Elite Eight of the NAIA National Playoffs this season. Luke feels blessed to be attending and playing football at such a great school.

The primary reason I shared Luke's accomplishments in the past couple of years is to emphasize an important point. A major lesson that fathers need to teach their children is to always work hard, be honest, keep their word, and maintain their character and integrity even when it is not easy and might not seem like the most popular thing to do. Typically, things tend to come full circle. Eventually, good things will happen to those who do things the right way. I am so pleased that my oldest son already has concrete evidence of this in his life. I am also very proud that he is proving to be a young man of virtue and good character. I am completely confident he will be a great future employee and a productive member of his community. Likewise, I am just as confident that when the right young lady comes along, he will make a wonderful husband and an awesome father to his children. I can't think of anything that would make me more proud as his dad!

Our second son, Cal, is fifteen years old and a freshman at Roncalli. He has a quick smile, a great sense of humor, and appears to be well liked in his class. One of life's great pleasures is to hear him laugh and chuckle when something strikes him as funny. Already, he has become a pretty well-established prankster, as he continually teases his mom and sisters in a good-natured way. He is quite witty and seems to enjoy verbally "jousting" with his friends. He also has the potential to become a pretty good football player. I am six foot two, and at fifteen years old, he is already taller than I am by about an inch and a half, and he weighs about 250 pounds. He is really pretty athletic for his height and size. Because of his sense of humor, he is a lot of fun to be around. I am really looking forward to coaching him for the next three years on the varsity team.

I am going to share one of my favorite Cal stories, because it makes a great final point about fatherhood. This story is from when Cal was about five years old. It was around Christmas, and the rest of the family had gone to bed. Once I had turned out all of the lights except for the Christmas tree, Cal snuggled up on my lap and laid his head on my chest (at his present size, I can hardly imagine holding him on my lap now!). After he had been still for several minutes, I assumed that he had fallen asleep. Staring at the Christmas tree lights, I had one of those delicious moments in time when I wanted to freeze everything so that I could just sit there for a long time and hold my son. Suddenly, Cal's head popped up. He looked at the tree for several seconds and then asked me a question I'm sure had been eating away at him for several minutes. "Daddy, do you think Santa Claus could beat up Jesus?"

Knowing this had probably been bothering him for a good long while, I knew that this was one of those rare opportunities that a father seldom has to say something profound that could change his son's life forever. So, I thoughtfully replied, "Aw, no way, Cal. It wouldn't even be close!" He was so astounded by my infinite wisdom that he immediately put his head back on my chest and was sawing logs within about sixty seconds.

This episode confirmed two things in my mind. First, Cal must have really wanted me, as his father, to tell him that even Santa Claus wouldn't stand a chance against Jesus. Faith formation is one of the primary tasks God gives to us as parents. As the man of our house, God depends on us to help our children find their way back to him. Deep down, I think our children want us to guide them on this journey. If we do a good job with this, in turn, they will guide their children along the same path. I will discuss this further in an upcoming chapter. The second thing this episode confirmed was how lucky and blessed I am to have two sons to call my own. I pray that God will always help me to be a strong and loving father to them both and a good role model that they can always look up to. When my sons were born, I knew that I would love them always with all my heart. I had always dreamed of having sons of my own, and they are both perfect gifts from God. They have both been an endless source of love, pride, and joy.

Finally, as fathers, one of the best ways we can show our children that we love them is to let them know that we will always be there for them and that they can count on us to keep our word. Whether it is attending sporting events, Christmas programs, helping with homework, or just being there when they want to talk, it is important for our children to know that they are a priority in our lives.

On December 7, 1988, a 6.9 earthquake hit Armenia, killing over thirty thousand people in less than four minutes. In the midst of this chaos, a father rushed to the school where his son was supposed to be. Once there, he saw that the school had collapsed into a pile of rubble. As the father looked at the hopeless situation, and as he saw dozens of other parents mourning the loss of their children, he remembered a promise he had made to his son: "No matter what, I'll always be there for you!" As tears filled his eyes, he knew what he had to do. He began focusing on where he walked his son to class each morning. Recalling that his son's classroom was in the back right corner of the building, he rushed there and started digging through the rubble.

After he had dug for awhile, some of the parents began to say, "You are too late. They are dead; you can't help. It's time to go home."

To each parent, he responded with one comment: "Are you going to help me now?" Then he proceeded to dig for his son, stone by stone.

As time passed, the fire chief showed up and tried to pull him from the debris, saying, "Fires are breaking out, and explosions are happening everywhere. You are in danger; you need to go home."

To this, the man replied, "Are you going to help me now?" He dug for twelve hours … eighteen hours … and finally a day had passed. People pleaded with him to go home. He was hungry and exhausted, but the promise he had made to his son continued to burn in his soul. So he continued to dig for twenty-eight hours … thirty-two hours … thirty-six hours … and then, in the thirty-eighth hour, he pulled back a stone and heard his son's voice. With his heart filled with emotion, he called out his son's name. He heard his son say proudly, "See, I told you so. I told you my dad would never stop looking until he found us!" Fourteen out of thirty-three of his classmates had survived, and the boy insisted that he be the last to be pulled from the rubble, because he knew that his father would never leave him there.

This is a good time for us to ask ourselves…would our children have this much faith in us being there for them under similar circumstances?

My children inspire me to strive to be the type of man they want me to be … a real man. So much of what I have done in my adult life has been done with the intent to make them proud—proud that I am their father and proud that they are my children. I do realize that I am truly blessed to have these four very special gifts from God as such a vital part of my life. I can only pray that they are as proud of me as I am of them.

Overtime

As the head football coach at Roncalli High School, I have been more than fortunate. During my time here, we have been blessed to win six state championships and one state runner-up title, all for which I have received beautiful rings. I also have a state runner-up ring for the last season I was the head track coach at Lawrence Central High School before coming to Roncalli. In addition, I have a couple more nice rings that I received when we won consecutive state championships. In all, I have ten rings commemorating wonderful experiences that I was blessed to be a part of.

After our last state championship, the new ring arrived. Since it is custom made, it is really a beautiful ring. My children were admiring it, and Luke asked, "Dad, which of the rings you've won means the most to you?" I thought this was an interesting question, and I chose this opportunity to make a point to my children. For the first time ever, I took all of the rings out of their boxes and put all of them on different fingers. Then I told them, "Now, I'm going to take these off one by one until I get to the one that means the most to me—the one that most represents hard work, loyalty, sacrifice, and accomplishment." After that, I began to take each of them off, putting them back in their boxes—pausing long enough so that they could see some of the years and so that I could pique their curiosity. When there was one state ring left on my hand, I quickly covered it with my other hand, took it off and put it in the box before anyone could see what year it was.

Luke protested, "Dad, we didn't get to see which one means the most to you!" To this, I replied, "Yes, you did, because I still have it on." At this point, I raised my left hand, where my wedding band was on my ring finger. "This is the ring that means the most to me. It represents years of hard work, loyalty, sacrifice, and accomplishment. It is, by far, the ring I am the most proud of and the one I never take off!" I'm not sure this was the answer they were looking for. Regardless, I wanted them to know that there is nothing in my life that I am prouder of than the fact that I am married to their mother. I believe this is one of the best ways for me to show my love for them.

I can remember my own mother telling me when I was younger that I could never know the fullest extent of love until I had children of my own. As always, my mom knew what she was talking about! I often pray that God will help me to always be a strong and loving role model in my children's lives. In doing so, I hope that they will always know how much I love them and how very proud I am to be their father.

CHAPTER 4

The Essence of Coaching

I LOVE ATHLETICS. I always have, and I always will. There is hard work and reward; setbacks and successes; determination, courage, loyalty, sacrifice, fighting for a common cause, and an endless list of other "lifetime lessons" to be learned on a daily basis. I am currently in the middle of my thirty-first year of coaching high school athletics. A primary reason I have committed most of my adult life to this endeavor relates to the wonderful experience I had as an athlete in my earlier years. They say that the more inclined we are to talk about ourselves, the less inclined people are to want to listen. Accordingly, I am going to share briefly my background in athletics to relate why I have continued to devote my professional career to this area.

I grew up in the middle of a family of eight kids. Since I grew up out in the country several miles from school, and both my parents worked full time, transportation was an issue. I did not play an organized sport until I played football, basketball, and ran track in eighth grade. I continued to play all three sports during my four years of high school. At the time, I had no idea of the tremendous impact athletics would ultimately have on my life. Prior to eighth grade, I had been somewhat shy and awkward at school. I soon

33

began to appreciate the fact that being an athlete gave me a new sense of identity and purpose, which resulted in newfound confidence and self-esteem. I also began to develop some very close friendships with my teammates. Early on, I began to understand the powerful influence that coaches have on the young people with whom they work. I quickly realized that the men I played for impacted my work ethic, my ability to work with others, and my overall attitude more than any other people in my life besides my parents.

I was blessed to enjoy some success as an athlete. I received a football scholarship to Butler University in Indianapolis. I loved playing college football. I started my sophomore, junior, and senior years at tailback and was able to set three school rushing records in the process. I think I made a good impression on the coaches, as I was the recipient of the Hilton U. Brown Mental Attitude Award after my senior year. Of all of the awards I received as an athlete, this is the one of which I am most proud. A few years ago, I was inducted into the Butler University Athletic Hall of Fame. There—I am now done bragging about myself.

The reason I shared this information is to make a point. I am certainly proud of my accomplishments as an athlete, but I have grown to realize that there is so much more to athletics than getting our names in the paper, winning games, setting records, or earning trophies, rings, or championships. Initially, striving for these things is good if it motivates us to set goals and work hard. However, in the grand scheme of things, these really are not the most important reasons to play. Athletics tend to be a microcosm of life. The lessons mentioned at the start of this chapter are life changing, and they play a much stronger role in affecting the people we become than any accolades won. I was certainly blessed to be coached by some outstanding gentlemen both at Plainfield High School and Butler University. It was through their influence and "life lessons" taught that I ultimately made the decision to become a teacher and coach as my chosen career. I entered this profession with a strong desire to have the same profound influence on young lives that these coaches had on mine. This is a decision I have never regretted.

In my time as a head coach, my goals and priorities have certainly evolved. As a young head coach, I used to dream of developing young men into all-state football players and ultimately turning them into unstoppable teams. Winning multiple state championships was at the top of my priority list. In more recent years, trying to accomplish these things is still important, but they have moved down my list of priorities. Don't get me wrong—every coach on our staff works extremely hard to watch and break down film, as well as creating the best game plan possible and working as hard as we can to get our guys ready to win games. I am just as passionate and devoted, if not more so, to these aspects of the game than I have ever been in my career. However, today I feel like I have a better grasp of the true responsibility of a coach. I now believe that every coach has two jobs they need to perform to be successful. The first, and most obvious, is to teach young people how to play a game. Every coach wants to teach his players how to run faster, jump higher, throw and kick better, and so on. In the same vein, it is certainly a coach's job to teach the rules and strategies of the game. Teaching kids how to play and win is very worthwhile, but I firmly believe that the next task is far more important and also more difficult. The main job of a coach is to teach his players how to live their lives and how to strive to be the kind of people God created them to be. When this is done well, this is by far the most rewarding of a coach's responsibilities, and it should be regarded as the priority in coaching.

It is estimated that around forty million kids play youth sports in America today. A majority of them are coached at these lower levels by parents of the players. Another seven million American teenagers play high school sports. Whether we are parents coaching our children in little league or high school or college coaches who do it for a living, there are some coaching concepts we need to consider. I spoke earlier of the "lifetime lessons" learned through athletics and how they can have a profound influence on the rest of our lives. Accordingly, I believe that when we accept the title of coach, no matter at what level, we should make the commitment to be a "lifetime coach."

There are three areas of development for which we as coaches are responsible. These areas are physical, mental, and spiritual. Initially, as coaches, our concerns must deal with physical improvement. For health reasons and for their safety, we need to have our kids in shape and ready to play. However, too many coaches put all of their emphasis on weightlifting, wind sprints, agilities, conditioning, and other physical activities to get ready for a game or season. This is where the philosophy of coaching to be a "lifetime coach" becomes important. Consider this—today, most kids begin playing team sports somewhere around third grade (some start sooner, some later). A vast majority of these kids will not play beyond high school, even though many of them might think they will. Thus, we are looking at around ten years that most kids play team sports. Interestingly, during these grade school and high school years, being socially successful is very closely associated with physical gifts with which we have been blessed. Think about this—during these years, being popular (which equates to success at this age) pretty much all ties in with physical gifts. Those who are the best looking (both male and female) and those who are most athletic tend to be the most popular (successful) kids in school. After high school, this begins to change. Although the physically gifted might still have some advantages, success begins to equate more with mental and educational development. You do not have to be good looking or athletic to be a doctor, lawyer, architect, pharmacist, dentist, teacher, or a CEO of a successful company. The careers we hold in the middle part of our lives tend to be much more associated with our mental development. Ultimately, what we do for a living will determine the size home we live in and the type of car we drive (which many Americans equate with success). Obviously, success in the middle and latter stages of life is more directly related to our education and our mental capabilities.

The average life expectancy in America today is around seventy-eight years old. If most athletes are done playing competitively at age eighteen, and we subtract that from a life expectancy of seventy-eight, we are looking at sixty years of mental development we need to be concerned with if we are going to be "lifetime coaches." As we compare the ten years that most play competitive sports to the sixty years of our lives after sports, where should our priorities be as a real coach? Mental development of our players extends beyond just teaching them to study hard and get good grades. It also includes teaching proper attitude, determination, and mental toughness. We need to teach our players that hard work correlates with success and that when we set our minds to something, quitting is not an option. Teaching our athletes how to deal with adversity is one of our biggest jobs, because they will face it for the rest of their lives. I tell our football players that as they learn that a bloody nose doesn't really hurt that badly, they are taking steps toward manhood. We encourage our sophomores who are getting their tail ends whupped each day in practice to get back up, dust themselves off, and get right back at it. One of the greatest joys in coaching football is watching our younger players go through this process. It is like a light switch clicks on when they figure out, "Hey, if I bounce back up and give everything I have and don't back down, bloody noses really don't hurt that bad. I *can* hang in here and go toe to toe with this senior!" As a coach, you can almost see that light switch click on when it happens. The neat thing is that, from that point on, the young man's life has changed forever! Everything else he will face for the rest of his life will seem easy. He has just taken a huge step toward manhood.

Obviously, a true "lifetime coach" will keep the ten years of physical development compared to sixty years of mental development in perspective as he creates priorities for his program. Now, let's go a step further. What happens on the day that athlete dies and passes from this earth? What have I, as his "lifetime coach," done to prepare him for eternity? When we compare ten years to sixty years, and then compare both of these to eternity, if we are trying to get our players ready for the rest of their lives, where should our priorities be? Have we prepared them to be successful in their lives beyond this world?

Each year, I make sure that our coaches are all on the same page in regard to our priorities for our football program. A majority of the coaches on our staff actually played for us in the past, so they are already on board and fully understand our expectations. Our staff has four priorities for our program. Priority #1 is faith development of our players and guiding them on their paths to eternity. Football is a physical and oftentimes violent game. Ironically, some of the toughest and most hard-nosed men I've ever known were at the same time deeply spiritual men. I first began to understand this while I was playing in college. Bill Sylvester, our head coach at Butler, was a faith-filled man. He never tried to push his beliefs on us, but we all respected the fact that he did not cuss in front of us (which is unusual for a lot of college coaches), and he led us in prayer before every game. Each Saturday, he would pray, "Lord, help us to remember that nothing is going to happen today that you and I together can't handle." He would always remind us as we were getting ready to take the field to "Play every play like a man in God's eyes." This concept would always bring tears to my eyes, and a tingle would run up my spine. I would pray like crazy that God would be with me and grant me strength and courage, and I could always feel his presence. As a ball carrier, I was not the fastest guy in the world. I was a lot more inclined to try to run over someone than around him. But one thing was for sure—when I allowed God in my heart, I was *not* afraid! I was always hurdling, diving, and crashing full speed into piles. Friends would tell me that I was crazy and would probably end up getting seriously hurt, because I had no regard for my body. That never happened. Regardless, I always felt God's presence, almost as if I had a shield of armor protecting me each Saturday afternoon. Along with feeling protected, I also felt a deep sense of duty and obligation. If I was going to pray to God and ask for his protection, I felt it was my duty each week to give him my best and that I was obliged to make the most of the gifts with which he had blessed me. I desperately wanted to make him proud! I always believed that I owed him that much.

As a coach, I try to instill these same principles in our players. Every kid wants to get his name in the paper the next morning after a game for scoring a touchdown. Boys always want the pretty girls up in the stands to notice them, and they will almost always want to make their parents proud. Every young man will play for these reasons. However, I have found that when we get our kids to understand that they are also playing for a higher purpose, extraordinary things begin to happen. That initially begins by creating a sense of family within our program. I can think of nothing that creates passion and emotion as much as our faith and our families. When we mix these two together, great things happen!

I have used this example before as I have spoken at coaching clinics. It is a bit barbaric, but it makes a good point. Imagine that you are at a social gathering with friends, and someone suddenly announces, "There is a 320-pound behemoth outside, and he is really ticked off. Someone has dented his new car, and he is furious. He wants someone to step outside and fight him!" Now, most people, unless they had been drinking heavily, would not volunteer for this detail. However, what if someone were to announce that this same behemoth was outside, and he had our parents, spouse, and kids out there and was going to beat them severely if we did not immediately come out and fight him? How long would it take us to get outside and take him on full speed ahead? This is the concept I share with our players about creating a "football family." With faith at the core, creating a sense of family becomes easier. I like the saying, "The family that prays together stays together." I heard Lou Holtz once say that as a college coach, he always tried to recruit young men with a faith background. He said, "People of faith care about others. They are inclined to help others; they are not only interested in their own personal gain. This is a big part of who they are. However, people who do not have a faith foundation tend to be in it for themselves. They don't really care about others and are only interested in what is best for them. Now, what type of young man do you want in your huddle on game day?" This concept, along with trying to prepare our players for eternity, ties in with faith development being the top priority in our program.

There are several things we do to promote faith development. We pray with our players after every practice and before and after every game. One of the first things we do is to teach our kids how to pray. I tell our players that when we pray, we should first give thanks for the many blessings in our lives. We should next pray for others. We all know many people who have issues in their lives, whether they are health, financial, or relational problems. I think it is good to ask God to be with others before we pray for ourselves. I also tell them that we should never pray for victory, because I really don't think God cares who wins football games. However, I think He does care that we try each day to give our best to make the most of the gifts He has blessed us with. Asking God to grant us the courage and wisdom to never take these gifts for granted is worthwhile! The first couple days of practice, our coaches will lead the team in prayer. We then turn it over to our players and let them volunteer each day to take the lead. Our players always do a great job with this. It is awesome to observe our guys as they stand in front of their peers, communicating with God and sharing something as intimate as prayer with their "brothers." This is always the first step in creating a "football family."

We do not allow cussing in our program. In my mind, when we are working with young people, there is no good reason to do it. We ask our players to control their emotions and behavior, so I feel we as coaches need to model this same discipline. Again, football is a very aggressive and demanding sport. If a player, out of frustration, allows a cuss word to slip out, we simply say, "Take off." They know that the punishment is a lap around our football and baseball field, which is at least a half-mile. If a coach accidentally slips, he does not have to run immediately, but he will get his lap in after practice is over. Our players enthusiastically remind him of his obligation. This might happen once a season.

The bottom line is that we don't allow cussing. In my mind, it demonstrates a lack of discipline!

Something else we do toward faith development is weekly Senior Scripture. Every Thursday night, this is the last thing we do to end our week of preparation. A senior will pick out a scripture verse from the Bible and share it with the team, tying it in with what is most important to him or our theme for the week. He will then lead us in a closing prayer. Normally, he will tape it to the inside of his locker for the rest of the season for inspiration. We also pray before every game. I allow each of our assistant coaches to sign up to give a pregame talk during the season. They always do a great job with this, and the kids enjoy hearing from them. Afterward, as we come into a tight huddle, with the players touching their helmets overhead, I always remind them to take God with them on every play. We always encourage them to say a quick prayer before every play. Maybe they ask for intensity or focus or courage on that given play. The key is that we want them to allow God in their hearts on every play. Karl Barth, the well-known Swiss theologian said, "Courage is fear that has said its' prayers." I believe this holds true in all facets of life, but it takes on very special meaning as it relates to a sport as physical and violent as football. Bob Nelson, motivational speaker and author once said, "You get the best effort from others not by lighting a fire beneath them, but by building a fire within." As coaches, our greatest challenge is to figure out the best way to light the fire of passion within each of our players. For many of our athletes, it is not so much the competition that exists with our opponents, but rather the battle each player wages within. It is our job to help our players claim victory over this "battle within." Until they have mastered the ability to conquer the self-imposed weaknesses of fear, fatigue, stress and self-doubt, they won't stand a chance against a formidable outside opponent. I have always believed the primary spark that ignites this internal flame has its' origin in our faith. This can be such an unbelievable source of strength and courage throughout the game. With this in mind, the final thing we do before we leave the locker room is "build the fortress." In a tight huddle, with the players' helmets touching overhead, I will recite St. Patrick's prayer, line by line, and they will repeat after me, "Christ behind me, Christ before me, Christ under my feet, Christ beside me, Christ over me. Let all around me be Christ." As we recite this, I will look our seniors right in the eyes, and most of them are emotional and ready to do something special. As our players take the field with God in their hearts, I am confident that they are going to give us everything they have. This is the concept of playing for a higher purpose. When an athlete is inspired by this belief in his heart, he can accomplish extraordinary things. I have seen it happen over and over again through the years!

Again, the reason we place such a high emphasis on faith development relates to the ten-years-versus-sixty-years-versus-eternity concept. Accordingly, as a "lifetime coach," faith development of our players will always be the first priority. Our second priority is character development. We want our players to be good people and to be leaders in our school and community. Our players know that if they want to play for us, they must conduct themselves as good role models. One year, I suspended one of our senior captains from his senior homecoming game for misbehaving in school. Although it might not have been a popular decision, it was the right decision. We want our players to know that they are accountable for their actions, and that as football players, they are being watched closely by others. We want them to love, respect, and honor their parents through their actions. We want them to grow to be men of character and of service to others and to be devoted and faithful husbands to their future wives. Likewise, we want them to be loving fathers to their children. I want all of our coaches to model these behaviors, as well. Oftentimes, we may not know for many years what kind of influence we have had on our players, but we often do receive good indicators. As we see that young man, maybe ten or twelve years later, standing along the fence at our game, holding his four-year-old daughter's hand, we know that we have done a good job of being "lifetime coaches." These are moments that are quite gratifying.

The third priority of our program is for our players to get a great education. Academics are strongly emphasized, as this directly relates to the sixty or so years of our lives after we are done playing. As mentioned earlier, our successes during our adult lives depend upon our academic preparation. I remind our players that in my twenty-one years as the head coach at Roncalli, we have only had one young man be drafted and actually have a career in the NFL. Statistics show that less than 1 percent of high school athletes will ever make it to the professional level. Only the most elite get that opportunity. Thus, our educations are what will determine our career choices and opportunities for the rest of our lives. Obviously, as "lifetime coaches," we need to continually stress the importance of academics to our athletes, regardless of the level at which we are coaching.

Finally, the fourth of our coaching priorities is that we want our players to be good athletes. Interestingly, what I have found over the years is that if we do a good job with the first three priorities, our kids are going to become pretty good football players! If they have faith, character, and work hard in the classroom, they will have great attitudes and work ethics. Ultimately, this will transfer over to success in athletics. Through my years of coaching, I have learned that three things are necessary to have great teams. You must have *talent*, good team *chemistry*, and your athletes must play with *passion*. The more you have of each of these qualities, the more games your team will win. Of these three characteristics, chemistry and passion are most closely linked. I have found that the teams that play with the most passion are loyal, have players who like one another, do not have key players who are in it for themselves, and make a strong effort to show respect for the coaches and each other. These teams are also, by far, the most fun to coach, regardless of win-loss records. Every school, unless they are able to go out and actively recruit top players, will have years where the talent pool is not as good. This tends to be cyclical. The most obvious indicator of this is how the eighth-grade classes from your feeder schools did four years earlier against their competition. Every class that comes through is going to have some talent. The difference is that some classes don't have the depth of talent you need to play at the most competitive levels. This is especially important in football, where you need to come up with twenty-two game-ready starters, as well as many special team members. A team might have a few great players, but if they lack depth of talent, they will struggle to beat the best teams on their schedule. Certainly, a good strength and conditioning program can help develop the athletes we have to an extent. However, all of the good teams we'll face during the season will be doing the same with their players. The bottom line is that some years we will not have the depth of talent that we do in others. It is during these years that great team chemistry, which leads to kids playing with great passion, is most important.

I believe that at the core of great chemistry among teammates is a profound sense of playing for a higher purpose, something far more important than ourselves. As coaches, we must convince our players that as they take the field, they are representing their school, community, family, friends, and God. We must continue to convince the young people in our charge that they can always do more, that they always have more to give, and that we believe in them. There is an old saying, "I don't care how much you know until I know how much you care." They need to know that we truly want them to be champions, both in the sport they play and in their daily lives. We work them hard to build their bodies so that they might achieve success in the game we coach. We must continually ask ourselves, "Where are we devoting most of our time and energy in developing our athletes? What are we doing to build their minds, hearts, and souls for the game of life and beyond?" As we coach in a way to teach our athletes how to live their lives long term, we will begin to see immediate results in our team chemistry and their willingness to play with passion and band together for a common cause. This happens best when we convince our players to take God with them on every play. Once this happens, we will never have a losing season! These are the lessons best taught by a "lifetime coach."

Joe Paterno, the longtime and much revered head coach at Penn State, was once asked by a reporter, "Coach, what kind of team are you going to have this year?" Coach Paterno wisely answered, "I don't know. Let's take a look at the kind of men these guys become twenty-five years from now before we answer that." Obviously, Coach Paterno gets it! Through his many years of coaching young men, he certainly has gained the wisdom of understanding the role of a real coach.

Finally, as we have discussed the role of a coach, let's consider the true measure of a coach. It is not so much about building great teams, but is really a lot more about building great young men. The true measure is not how many rings, plaques, and championship trophies are won. Instead, it is about how many men out of how many boys. I now realize that when I have coached my last game and the last whistle is blown, I will not look at the scoreboard to see how many points were scored for their team versus how many points were scored for ours. Instead, I will look at the scoreboard in my heart to see the score that matters most—*how many lives have I touched and changed for the better?* This is how I can best measure success and where I will find my greatest reward. This, I believe, is the true *essence of coaching*.

Overtime

Over the years, I have periodically reflected on the additional income I could have made if I had gone into another profession. Almost all of my buddies from both high school and college now have higher incomes and consequently live in larger homes, drive newer cars, can afford nicer clothes, and so on. As our children have gotten older, this has become even more pronounced as Jackie and I consider car insurance for four teenagers, grocery bills, upcoming college costs, and preparing for eventual retirement, along with other financial concerns that middle-aged couples must deal with. A few years back, a friend talked with me about a career change. He threw around some pretty impressive numbers for potential income if I went to work for his company. Suddenly, he asked, "What do you make teaching and coaching at a parochial school?"

Compared to some of the numbers he had been discussing, I was at first a little embarrassed to answer this question. But, after contemplating for five or six seconds before answering, I said, "I make a difference!" I went on to explain that I believe that God placed me at Roncalli for a reason, and that by working hard each day to teach and influence the lives of young people, I was doing exactly what he was calling me to do. I think my buddy really understood for the first time my decision to stay teaching and coaching at Roncalli, and he has never brought up the subject again.

Choosing to be a parochial school educator, I know that I will never be wealthy or rich with material possessions. But I also know that I love my wife, I love my children, I love my God, I love the young people I work with each day, and I love what I do for a living. Consequently, in so many ways, in the most *important* ways, I consider myself to be one of the wealthiest men I know! God has blessed my life in so many ways, and I pray that He will always grant me the wisdom to never take these blessings for granted. As I strive each day to live my life as a real man, I hope that God will also help me each day to be a real coach, a true "lifetime coach."

Back in the day. This is me taking a handoff in a game at Butler University. My involvement in athletics played a huge role in my development as a man.

CHAPTER 5

Season of Angels

WE WERE BLESSED to become the first team from Indiana to win three consecutive 4A state championships in football. This is the second-largest class in the tournament, and we won consecutively in 2002, 2003, and 2004. After the '04 season, several people approached me and said, "Someone needs to document some of the unbelievable things that have happened during these past three years." They were right. That winter, I wrote my first book entitled *Beyond the Goal Line: The Quest For Victory in the Game of Life.* I wrote the book for our Roncalli community, and I included countless local names of people who had touched my life in my time at Roncalli High School. I self-published the book and had two thousand copies printed. We sold them primarily at our football games the next fall, and they sold out quickly. Although the book was written primarily for our school community at that time, I have decided to include one chapter about the 2002 season in this book. I think it ties in with the topic of the last chapter, "The Essence of Coaching," and it will also serve as a nice transition into our next chapter. This was the chapter entitled "Season of Angels."

The phone rang. It woke me from a deep sleep. As I reached to answer it, I glanced at the clock, which read 1:09 a.m. Immediately,

I wondered who in the world would be calling me at that time of night. On the other end was Ricky Clevenger, one of our players who had just finished his sophomore year. Fighting back tears, he informed me that Jonathan Page, his classmate and one of his best friends, had been in a serious automobile accident. He told me it was pretty bad and wanted to know if I could come to the hospital to be with the family. I told him I'd be right there. It was Monday, June 3, 2002.

Jonathan was a handsome, witty young man with a wonderful and somewhat mischievous smile. He was the fastest kid in his class and an excellent football player. In fact, the coaching staff was counting on him to be a starter the following season as either a defensive back or a flanker—perhaps even both.

On his freshman team, Jonathan had been the leading ball carrier and was voted co-MVP by his teammates. However, he was one of the few players in our program who hadn't attended one of our south side Catholic grade schools. He had attended Center Grove Middle School, a large school system south of Roncalli. In spite of having a very successful first semester at Roncalli, Jonathan decided to transfer to Center Grove for the start of the second semester. He told me he had just missed his old middle school friends too much. He went on to run track that spring at Center Grove.

The next fall, Jonathan showed up on the third day of two-a-day practices, wanting to know if he could come back to Roncalli and be a part of the team. He stood in front of the squad and explained that as soon as he transferred, he knew he had made a mistake. He realized how much he loved and missed Roncalli football and wanted to know if we would accept him back. I informed him that it wouldn't be easy. Since he had played a spring sport at Center Grove, the transfer back would mean he wouldn't be eligible for varsity play. He could, however, practice with us and play in the junior varsity games in the upcoming season.

As one of our "scout team" running backs, in practice Jonathan always went hard and took an incredible pounding, and yet he was talented and tough, never complained and never backed down from heavy contact. By season's end, he had won the respect of every player and coach in the program. Since he would be eligible for varsity play the next fall, he had everyone convinced he would be one of our best players in his junior year.

As I arrived at the hospital, several of Jonathan's family and friends were already there. Father Tom Clegg, our school priest, came out and informed me that Jonathan's parents, Scott and Holly Page, were in his room and wanted me to come pray with them. Jonathan was in a coma, had several tubes and wires connected to various parts of his body, and was hooked to a ventilator. I was immediately struck by how much he had to labor to take each breath. After visiting and praying with Scott and Holly, Father Tom gathered several of the football players who were there and recommended we "build the fortress" like we do before every game by joining hands with Scott and Holly, forming a circle around Jonathan's bed, and reciting St. Patrick's prayer. The words "Christ behind me, Christ before me, Christ under my feet, Christ beside me, Christ over me, let all around me be Christ" had never held a stronger meaning or intent. I definitely felt the presence of Jesus in the room that night.

Like a warrior, Jonathan refused to surrender and continued to fight for his life. Living longer than expected, he passed away two days after his accident. As I went to visit the family, Scott asked if Steve Wilson, our head freshman coach, and I would do the eulogy. Knowing that it would be one of the most difficult things I have ever done in my coaching career, I replied that I would be honored.

The day before the funeral, calling was held at the Catholic church the family attended to allow Jonathan's many friends and loved ones to pay their respects. As Jackie and I made our way forward, I asked her to kneel and pray with me by the casket. When I gazed at Jonathan's handsome face, I noticed he had a football tucked under his forearm, and on his chest was a picture of him carrying the football in a Roncalli game. I was suddenly overcome with emotion and began to weep openly. In the twenty-three years I had known Jackie, this was the only time she had seen me cry. However,

I was neither ashamed nor embarrassed. I had grown to love this young man because of his courage, personality, and warrior's heart. I could only imagine the heartache his parents were enduring.

At Jonathan's funeral the next day, the church was full of family and friends who had come to celebrate his life and mourn his passing. As a show of solidarity, players and coaches from Chatard, Cathedral, Scecina, and Ritter, all rival Catholic schools, were in attendance. The largest group, other than Roncalli, were the players from Center Grove, who in many instances had known Jonathan since grade school. To further underscore their unity that day, all of the players from each of the schools were wearing their jerseys.

Steve Wilson gave his part of the eulogy first and did a wonderful job of paying tribute to Jonathan. As I was approaching the lectern to give my part of the eulogy, I prayed that God would grant me courage to get through it, wisdom to appropriately reflect on Jonathan's life, and enough compassion to let Scott and Holly know how lucky their son was to have them as parents.

I began by thanking all those in attendance, especially the players and coaches from the other schools. I went on to say there were three things I would always remember about Jonathan. The first was his courage. The resolve he showed in leaving Roncalli, then coming back to receive a tremendous pounding without ever complaining was remarkable. His courage carried over to his time in the hospital as he fought like a warrior for his life. His courage would always be remembered.

The second thing I stated was that I would never forget his mischievous smile and his sense of humor. Beyond his good looks and great athletic talent, he was a wonderful young man. I told Scott and Holly that he was a beautiful reflection of them, and that he knew how much they loved him. Likewise, he loved them very much, was proud to be their son, and was lucky to have them as his parents. I asked Scott and Holly to look around the room. The huge crowd was certainly a fine tribute to their son, but it was also a true reflection of both of them.

Finally, I would always remember the way Jonathan touched the lives of others. I shared that I had recently grown to believe the ultimate way we can give thanks to God for the countless gifts he has given us is to help bring others closer to him so we might all experience his life-changing love. I asked those in the church to reflect back on the events of the past week — the prayers sent to God, all of the love and support given to the Page family, and the different school communities that had all come together as one Christian family to honor a wonderful young man and his family. I finished by stating, "If, in fact, the greatest way to pay tribute to God is to use our gifts to bring other people closer to Him, I think this truly is Jonathan's finest hour! Jonathan, we thank you for that!" God had certainly answered my prayers and allowed me to get through the eulogy without breaking down. More importantly, I hope I was able to be a part of helping Scott and Holly give their precious son back to God.

When the funeral concluded, players from all the schools lined both sides of the long sidewalk from the church to the hearse to pay a final tribute to Jonathan as the coffin was carried past. Along with the Page family, I appreciated this show of support and unity from the other schools.

We began the summer mourning Jonathan's death; however, other concerns were being dealt with as well. In the spring of the previous school year, six upcoming seniors had been caught drinking at a party. These six included a few of our better players, some of whom had been projected to be starters. According to school policy, they would all be suspended for the first 2 ½ games of the season (25 percent of our regular schedule.) Our first four opponents were extremely tough. So, not having some of our best players available created a significant amount of worry. In addition to our roster problems, we had even more serious concerns since two of our players' fathers were battling cancer and struggling to cling to life.

Karl Andrews had graduated from Roncalli in the late 1970s where he met his lovely wife Robin. Bob Tully coached at Roncalli when Karl played and said he was one of the toughest, most hard-nosed players he's ever coached. Karl was from a family of sixteen kids and had to work very hard to help pay his tuition to Roncalli. He carried the same determined work ethic into his adult life. He was a loving husband to Robin and a wonderful father to his four children. Karl's oldest son, Nick, had played for us on our 1999 State Championship team and possessed many of his father's qualities, and his second son, Phil, was going to be a sophomore on the 2002 squad. Karl had many, many friends and was loved not only by his immediate family, but by all who knew him.

As the summer passed into early June, Karl's health continued to decline. Due to his extreme weight loss and the fact that he felt so poorly, only family members were permitted to see him. On June 23, 2002, he passed away while surrounded by his family. Given his lifelong love and passion for Roncalli football, our program had truly lost a strong member of the Roncalli family. For the second time that summer, our community was in mourning.

Despite the heartbreaking loss of two members of the Roncalli football family, we continued to prepare for the start of the season even with the knowledge that another member of our football family was fighting for his life. Dick Nalley, who had been the toughest college player I had come up against while at Butler, was in the final stages of his battle with cancer. As a running back at Roncalli in the early 1970s, he was the perfect combination of strength, speed, toughness, agility, and explosive power. He was named First Team All-State and Catholic All-American. Additionally, he set all of Roncalli's sprint records in track and would go on to set multiple rushing records at Indiana Central University in Indianapolis. After college, he came within 37/100ths of a second from winning the bronze medal in the 1980 Olympics at Lake Placid in the bobsled competition.

From a high school All-American to an Olympic hero, many old timers still say he was the best football player to ever to wear the Roncalli uniform. When I became friends with Dick as an adult, what I admired most about him was that he was a wonderful father to his two sons and two daughters. Richie, his oldest son, played a key role as a ball carrier on the 1999 team. He then became our leading rusher and scorer on the 2000 team. Marcus, Dick's younger son, was a three-year starter in our varsity backfield and was our starting tailback on both the 2001 and 2002 teams. Like his father, Marcus was extremely strong, fast, and explosive. At five feet eleven and 205 pounds, he ran a 4.55 forty-yard dash and could bench-press 360 pounds. Just like his father, he relished being a punishing runner.

Twenty-five years earlier, when I was competing against Dick at the collegiate level, I had no idea that his sons and nephews would become All-State running backs on the high school teams I would be coaching. As an athlete and a competitor, Dick always had an indestructible "Superman" persona about him. Even after his days as an Olympic athlete were over, he continued to participate in weightlifting competitions. With a body weight under two hundred pounds, he could still bench-press well over four hundred pounds and won several state power-lifting titles. Even as he approached middle age, he still carried a "larger than life" persona on the south side of Indianapolis.

Throughout the summer of 2002, cancer continued to weaken his once indestructible body. But being a warrior seems to run in the Nalley blood. He lived far beyond what his doctors had projected and made it very clear that one of his primary goals was to see his son play football again. It was a tremendous source of pride for Dick that his sons had followed in his footsteps to become star running backs for Roncalli. Through sheer courage, fortitude, and an iron will, he clung to life and was able to see his wish come true.

We opened the 2002 season at Center Grove, a team that has become a 5A powerhouse in Indiana football. Both teams lined up on their respective forty-five-yard lines before the game. In honor of Jonathan, a tribute was read over the intercom, a few moments of silence were observed, and finally several balloons were released. It was a wonderful tribute to Jonathan and a fitting way to start the season.

As the game began, our offense sputtered a bit because of the suspensions and a couple of injuries among key players. Marcus played his heart out and ultimately scored our only touchdown of the night as we lost our hard-fought season opener 14–7. I was in the press box waiting for the post-game radio interview when I saw three or four men slowly moving down the steps. After a closer look, I could see they were huddled around Dick, who was carefully making his way out of the stadium. Since I hadn't seen him for a few weeks, I was shocked at how thin and frail he seemed. At the time, it didn't occur to me that this would be the last time I would see him inside a football stadium.

The next week, we prepared for our game against Franklin Central, and I knew we were going to have our hands full. On film, this team reminded me a lot of the 1990 team coached by Chuck Stevens. Even though Marcus didn't want to talk about his dad's health, I had heard Dick was getting steadily worse. However, since it was one of his father's strictest rules, Marcus never missed practice. That Wednesday night, early in practice, Marcus' brother, Richie, pulled up to the practice field. I was at the far end of the field and didn't get to speak to either of them, but they both got in the car and left in a hurry. After practice that evening, we were notified that Dick had passed away. In less than three months, the Roncalli community would be burying another beloved member of our family.

When Marcus returned to school on Friday, there wasn't a moment's doubt whether he would be playing in the game that evening. Dick would have insisted that he not miss the game. That morning, Marcus came to see me to ask about changing his jersey number. In high school, he had always worn number 30 while his dad had worn 24 in high school and college. Marcus said, "Coach, I've never wanted to wear my father's number because I wanted to create my own identity and not play in his footsteps. Now, I want that to change. I want to run exactly in my father's footsteps to honor him. Can I switch my jersey number to 24?" At that point, he was doing a much better job keeping his eyes from welling up with tears than I was.

Wearing number 24 that night, Marcus ran like a man possessed. Due to the ongoing player suspensions, we were outmatched up front, and there was often nowhere to run. It was obvious, however, that Marcus was consumed with passion as he once again scored our only touchdown. We lost again that night, as we would the following week to a very good Chatard team. They scored in the last thirty seconds to win 14–10. In week four, we traveled to Cincinnati to play Elder, a big all-boys Catholic school that went on to win Ohio's largest class state championship that year. They pounded us pretty soundly and, for the first time as either an athlete or coach, I was sitting on a 0–4 record. It became very obvious that death is not a good motivator. Instead, it only serves to drain you—both physically and emotionally.

During the two-and-a-half-hour ride home from Cincinnati, I reflected on what this group of young men had dealt with over the previous four months. It occurred to me that our team was at a crossroads, and that our attitude and approach in the upcoming weeks would dictate how the rest of the season would turn out. I also knew that ultimately it was my responsibility to redirect this ship, which was adrift.

Since it was almost two o'clock in the morning by the time we had the buses unloaded and everyone gathered in the locker room, I decided to make my post-game remarks short and to the point. I said, "Fellas, right now, we are 0–4. Obviously, we have a lot of work to do. But, I've been around you long enough to know something about your character, and I know the families you come from! Seniors, I'm telling you right now, you will not lose another game in your high school football careers!" As the seniors made quick, sideways glances at each other, a look of determination and commitment occupied their faces. This resolve was exactly what we needed. I pulled them together for the closing prayer then sent them home.

I wasn't surprised when the team came out fired up for practice the next week. After a disappointing 0–4 start, unlike most groups, these guys were hitting and hustling with a vengeance. Adding fuel to the fire was the fact that we were to play Scecina on our home turf that week. We all knew we were in desperate need of a win, and this team felt a victory over a rival Catholic school at home could be the turning point in our season. When the school day began that Friday, they were chomping at the bit to play!

By lunch time, however, we were beginning to receive reports that a nasty storm was heading our way. The storm was heading for Indianapolis from the southwest and was bringing various tornado watches and warnings along with it. By one o'clock, the sky had taken on an ominous appearance, and the area was placed under a tornado watch. At 1:45, we were informed that a tornado had touched down and was heading directly toward the southeast side of the city, which meant Roncalli was in its path. We were also warned that it would arrive in the next fifteen minutes. In keeping with our emergency plans, we immediately gathered all one thousand students, faculty, and staff into the lower and middle hallways, and closed every door in the building.

By two o'clock, the wind was blowing so hard I was afraid the walls might collapse. Thankfully, within ten minutes, it had passed. Although we usually dismiss students for the day at 3:00, the state police called to let us know that a tornado had indeed passed through the neighborhood. We were told that area homes had been destroyed and power lines were down everywhere. The police also let us know that we should keep everyone in the building until some roadways could be cleared. Approximately three hours later, we were finally allowed to dismiss the students. The city was beleaguered; businesses were closed, transportation was impossible, and people scrambled to salvage what remained. As you may suspect, our game that night was cancelled.

As I walked through the parking lot, the scene around me was surreal. The neighborhood west of the school had been devastated. Large trees were down, entire roofs had been ripped off homes, and furniture and personal belongings were scattered everywhere. Several homes had been completely flattened with no walls standing. I had never seen anything like it before. Later, we found out the tornado had stayed on the ground for 112 miles—the second longest in

Indiana history. Miraculously, no one had been killed; however, the damage estimate throughout the area was over $50 million. The only noticeable damage to Roncalli was to two forty-foot pine trees, which had been uprooted from the circle at the front of the school. God must have been watching over the inhabitants of our school building that day!

As happy as I was regarding the safety of our school, I was concerned about the psychological state of our football team. We had fought through three devastating deaths, the suspensions of some key players, an 0–4 start, and now a tornado had cancelled game five. Going into the sixth week of the season, we were still winless. I was beginning to wonder just how much more this team could take.

To my amazement, they came out the following week more focused and energized than ever. They were convincing me they truly had what it took to be a championship team. That Friday night, we played one of the best games in my career as a coach when we defeated Elkhart Central, a 5A team from northern Indiana, 42–7. Marcus played an unbelievable game and rushed for 327 yards (a new school record) and five touchdowns in less than three-quarters of play. After starting 0–4, we won our last four regular season games by a combined score of 180–23.

After a convincing win in the sectional opener, we faced Cathedral on their home field exactly one year after they had beaten us there in overtime to end our season. Just like the year before, it was a classic "slug-fest." Our quarterback, Nick Johnson, hit Marcus out of the backfield for an eighteen-yard touchdown pass in the first quarter. Cathedral then put together a long scoring drive early in the second quarter to tie the score at 7 each. With the first half winding down, we tried to sustain a drive to put points on the board to hopefully take a lead into halftime.

Earlier that week, I was standing in class when Pat Kuntz, who had been a close friend of Jonathan's, approached me. He asked if it would be okay if he was a little late to practice that day, because he and a couple of friends wanted to go to Jonathan's grave after school to commemorate his birthday. Of course, I gave my approval, and as I turned around to the clipboard on my desk, I suddenly felt overwhelmed by a feeling of peacefulness throughout my body. I was drawn to the clipboard and wrote down an unusual, unbalanced shotgun formation with motion that we had never used before. As I look back now, I'm convinced that Jonathan's spirit had visited me and urged me to write down this bizarre formation and accompanying play. I installed the play in practice that week but had forgotten about it during the game.

Late in the second quarter, in a crucial situation, I felt Jonathan's presence again, so I decided to call Jonathan's play. It caught Cathedral by surprise as Marcus took off on a forty-two-yard gain. This set up a second touchdown for Marcus as we took a 14–7 lead into halftime.

We fought back and forth through the second half until Cathedral finally punched in a score with less than three minutes to play. Their PAT tied the score 14–all. Ironically, this had been the score the previous year on the same field at the end of regulation play. Although I felt prepared, I didn't want to go into overtime again— at this point, the momentum was on their side.

Starting with the ball on our twenty-seven-yard line with about two and a half minutes to play, I was hoping just to move the ball systematically down the field to set up a field goal. Instead, with about two minutes to go, Marcus found a slight seam, shot through the hole, and outran their defenders for a sixty-six-yard touchdown run. As he crossed the goal line, he looked up and pointed his finger to the sky. Although some in the crowd might have thought he was making the sign for "#1," everyone on our side knew to whom he was signaling. After the game, he told his mom that as he broke through the hole, he could see his father standing down past the end zone among the huge crowd. So, he ran right toward him. As he entered the end zone, his father was gone. I have no doubt that Dick's spirit was with Marcus that night as he rushed for 239 yards and scored all three touchdowns against a strong Cathedral defense.

After winning a hard-fought sectional championship over Shelbyville, we traveled to a very tough East Central team in the regional game. As is usual in Indiana in the fall, practice that week was cold and rainy, and the foul weather continued through game night. Even though East Central was a junior dominant team, they were very fast and physical. We took a 10–7 lead into the fourth quarter, but they kicked a field goal late in the game to send it into overtime. By now, the playing conditions were as miserable as any I had ever faced. The cold rain was blowing almost parallel to the ground, cutting like a razor as it hit your skin. Despite the conditions, neither team was ready to let down.

East Central won the coin toss and elected to play defense first. Even with a sore knee, Marcus pounded it in to take a 17–10 lead. East Central then had the ball on the ten-yard line going in and four downs to score. After a couple of unsuccessful runs, their quarterback began to scramble, looking to pass. He threw it out into the flats to his left, but David Oechsle, our outside linebacker, made a diving interception to end the contest and sent us to the semi-state game. The overtime loss was heartbreaking for East Central, and, since they had so many underclassmen starting, we knew they would be an awesome force to contend with the next season.

At this point, all of our energy had to be focused on getting ready for the upcoming semi-state game in which we would face the mighty Jasper Wildcats. This team was coached by Indiana's all-time winningest coach, Jerry Brewer, who was finishing a brilliant forty-four year career. His 368 wins were the most in Indiana history. The previous year, he had led Jasper to the 4A State Championship (his first as a head coach). Therefore, his team was determined to make it two in a row. Before the season began, Jerry had announced that he would retire at the end of the season—win or lose. Obviously, we knew his team was going to come into our place sky high and that it would be a very emotional game for both teams.

The offensive strategy of both schools was almost identical: power football out of the "I" backfield and a lot of power toss.

Three of their most highly skilled players were brothers—the quarterback and wide receiver were identical twins who were really fast and, as seniors, were a dangerous combination. Their younger brother was the tailback. Like Roncalli, their offense was very physical and run oriented—as most teams still playing at this point of the Indiana tournament are.

That night, Roncalli proved to be a little more durable, and we rushed sixty-four times for 240 yards compared to twenty-five Jasper attempts for 131 yards. Chris Belch and our defensive staff had done a masterful job preparing for Jasper's offense, holding them to six points. Marcus scored in the third quarter, followed by a Kevin Trulock field goal. At least half a dozen times in the third quarter, Marcus pounded ahead on third and short, or fourth and short, to pick up the first down by inches. His efforts allowed us to eat up the clock and barely hold onto a narrow 10–6 victory. Marcus certainly earned his keep that night with fifty carries (a new Roncalli record) and 179 yards rushing.

Interestingly, I had felt the distinct presence of our three angels prior to the game. It had rained just about every night that week, and, in an attempt to keep the field as dry as possible, we had put down several sheets of plastic every night after practice. Unfortunately, the plastic needed to be removed each day to allow the grass to "breathe." All week long, I spent my prep periods removing plastic—only to repeat the process the next day. This daily chore made me lose a lot of valuable game preparation time. When we cleared the plastic off for the last time on game day, I realized I was less prepared for this game mentally and organizationally than I had been for any game in my coaching career. The game field looked nice but, psychologically, I was a mess. Here I was getting ready to play against the defending state champions, and I was hopelessly unprepared.

About ninety minutes before game time, I felt like I was on the verge of having an anxiety attack. As I opened the door to my office, I noticed a large sign on the wall that I hadn't seen all week. In big, bold letters, it read, "WE ARE GUIDED BY ANGELS," followed by "24, 26, 31." which had been Dick, Jonathan, and Karl's jersey numbers. Suddenly, I felt the familiar warm, tingling sensation engulf my body. My heart rate immediately began to return to normal, and, for the first time all week, I actually felt calm and at peace. The feeling remained with me for the rest of the night—even through the numerous points of the game when our entire season was on the line. To this day, I believe our three angels produced that calm.

Prior to that season, I'm not sure I even believed in angels intervening in human affairs. But now, beyond a shadow of a doubt, I know it is true. In the past three years, I've had several other people share "angel stories" from that season—too many to write about in this book. I know the spirits of Jonathan, Karl, and Dick were with us that season.

I had coached in three state championship games prior to 2002, but this was our school's first trip in 4A football. Fort Wayne Dwenger, our opponent, was big, fast, aggressive, and exceptionally well coached. We knew we would have to execute in all three phases of the game to have a shot at winning. Dwenger boasted a 13–1 record compared to our 9–4 season. Interestingly, exactly twenty years earlier, Roncalli had played in the school's first state championship against Dwenger. Steve Wilson, our freshman coach, was the star running back on that Roncalli team. Early in the fourth quarter, Roncalli had held a 21–7 lead, but Dwenger came back late in the game to win it 22–21. At our 2002 championship game, there were many former Rebels in the crowd who wanted to even the score. Little did they know that, in many ways, this game would mirror that night twenty years before, with one important twist.

Roncalli opened the game by marching seventy-two yards on fourteen plays, consuming almost seven minutes of the clock. Nick Johnson hit our tight end, Jake McCoy, with a seventeen-yard touchdown pass to take a 7–0 lead. Midway through the second quarter, Kevin Trulock, hit a thirty-six-yard field goal to increase our lead to 10–0. Before the half, Dwenger responded with a sixty-eight-yard scoring drive to leave the score 10–7 at the half. In the third quarter, Dwenger carried their momentum into the opening drive with a sixty-six-yard march down the field to take the lead with a 14–10 score. Our offense began to sputter in the third quarter, and things began to look very bleak when Marcus was tackled on the sideline and heard a loud "pop" from his knee. Suddenly, we were faced with going into the fourth quarter without our best player. Marcus had rushed for over 2,300 yards, but as of that moment, he was done for the season. We were stunned and heartbroken.

Early in the fourth quarter, Dwenger scored again to take a 21–10 lead. Ironically, the sportswriters had projected us as eleven-point underdogs. With Marcus out of the game, it appeared they might be right. What they hadn't taken into account, however, was the warrior mentality of this team. We had fought through so much, and the entire team had taken a vow in our locker room at 2:00 a.m. after game four that our seniors weren't going to taste defeat again that season.

We trailed by eleven points with 9:25 left to play when Dwenger punted from midfield to our fifteen-yard line. D.J. Russell, our senior wide receiver, fielded the ball and returned it thirty yards to the forty-five yard line. We had inserted Tim Sergi, our starting free safety, who was a tall, fast, physical sophomore, as tailback to replace Marcus. I began to pray for focus, clarity, and peace of mind, and I think God granted all three. With Marcus out of the game, we went back to "Jonathan's offense," the unbalanced shotgun set with a lot of motion. Nick Johnson did a masterful job running the offense as we combined quick spot passes to Kyle Stephenson, a senior and one of the best athletes on the team, with backs motioning out of the backfield and periodic quarterback draws. Nick was a very deceptive runner on these draws and, after leading us on a fifty-five-yard drive, ended up doing a complete flip in the end zone following a four-yard run for the score.

With less than six minutes to play, we were trailing 21–17. Our defense really stepped up as Peter Szostak, our defensive end, made two consecutive tackles for a loss and forced our opponent into a three and out. We returned the punt to midfield with 4:25 to go.

Mixing formations, Tim Sergi ran with poise and determination not usually found in a sophomore—especially not one who had played almost the entire season on the other side of the ball. Facing fourth down and two from the fourteen-yard line with under two minutes to play, Tim slammed off left tackle on a toss play to pick up a first down on the five-yard line. His adrenaline surged as we gave it to him to the right for another four-yard gain. With one minute to play and the ball on the one-yard line, we were trailing by four points. The state championship was on the line, and the roar inside the RCA Dome was deafening.

We decided to run a power toss to the left—the weak side of the formation. Tim took the pitch, made one cut, and knifed into the end zone! The Rebel crowd went berserk, and I don't think I have ever heard a crowd in the dome that was that loud—before or since. Ahead by one, we punched in the two-point conversion off right tackle to take a 24–21 lead. Our defense held for four downs, and we took a knee to run out the clock. Just as Dwenger had done twenty years earlier, we had come from two scores down late in the fourth quarter to claim a state championship. This was the sixth in our school history and my fourth as the head coach.

At Roncalli that evening, we held a standing-room-only pep session in the gymnasium. After several words of thanks, I called Scott and Holly Page up on stage. I explained that we had kept Jonathan's name and jersey number on our roster for the entire season, because we knew he would be there with us in our hearts and souls for the duration of the season. I told them I had no doubt that at that very moment he was watching with that big, handsome smile on his face. I then told them I had a presentation I wanted to make. In a very emotional moment, I removed my state championship medal and placed it around Scott's neck and told him I wanted him to have it on Jonathan's behalf. Afterward, I gave both he and Holly long, heartfelt hugs.

Reflecting back on the 2002 season, I continue to pray for the families of Jonathan, Karl, and Dick. I know there is nothing we can ever do to bring back their loved ones. However, if in some small way, we allowed others to feel their presence, even for a few fleeting moments, all of our lives are richer because of it. I know their spirits were present in my life frequently during that season and, periodically, I am blessed with their presence yet today.

What continues to ring in my soul now is not the memory of the haunting phone call I received that bleak Monday morning so long ago. What rings now is the peace of knowing that I have been transformed somewhat by the presence of love ... the love that resounds in the joy through Jonathan Page, Karl Andrews, and Dick Nalley. Consequently, I know my life will never be the same.

Overtime

The 2002 season was a truly remarkable and memorable season. Though it forced all of us to deal with heartbreaking adversity, it also brought all of us to a stronger relationship with God. I know that I was blessed to be a part of it! Of all the chapters from my first book, this is the one that I chose to include as part of this follow-up book. I think it best illustrates that if we take time to look each day, we can find signs of God in our everyday lives. I think sometimes our faith is hard to define, especially to those who have trouble believing in something they can't touch or see. In some ways, I think our faith is like the wind. Although we can't really see it, we know it is there, we certainly at times feel it, and we see the results of its power. Luckily, when we find ourselves struggling with our faith, we periodically have people sent into our lives who become true models of faith. Through their examples, they help us to better understand the depth of God's love for us.

In the next chapter, we are going to take a detailed look at the strongest, toughest man who ever lived. He gained his strength and courage through his faith. Consequently, he became the most influential man to ever walk the face of the earth. Let's move into the next chapter and meet him!

Marcus Nalley crossing the goal line, pointing up to his father, Dick, who had the best seat in the house.

CHAPTER 6

A Real Man's Man

ACCORDING TO RECENT population polls, America today has right at 308 million people living within her borders. Recent polls also say that 83 percent of these people believe in God through one faith or another. More specifically, 76 percent, or 234 million Americans, report being of the Christian faith. Being raised within a Christian household, I am a proud member of this larger Christian family. An interesting perspective I've heard is that, if you were brought to trial for being a Christian, would there be enough evidence to convict you? When I was younger, there were probably stages in my life—of which I now might not be really proud—where this might have been in question. But I think those who have known me during my adult life would say that I would now easily be convicted. Again, I am very proud of this fact. I will never apologize for my religious beliefs.

In America, we are all allowed religious freedom. The framers of the Constitution guaranteed this. If people in this country choose not to believe in God or his son Jesus, I suppose it is their choice. However, being one of the 234 million Americans (a very obvious majority) that do believe, I will *always* say, "Merry Christmas," "In God we trust," and "One nation, under God," and I will always say, "God bless you" when someone sneezes. Being a member of such a clear-cut majority, I believe it is politically incorrect *not* to say those things! That's my right, and I can't help but wonder why it seems that we must be careful or apologetic for being Christians in a country like America where Christians are the clear-cut majority. OK, I'll get off my soapbox now.

Let's begin to look at the Christian faith in more detail. At the core of this religion is the bravest, strongest, and toughest man who ever lived. He roamed the earth about two thousand years ago. His name was Jesus. In America today, as a nation that is predominately Christian in faith, I think it is good to periodically reflect on the life of Jesus. His life and his teachings have been more influential on America and many other parts of the world than any other person in the history of mankind. What we know of Jesus' life comes mostly from the four Gospels, the first four books of the New Testament.

He was born of humble means in a stable in Bethlehem. He spent most of his life in the town of Nazareth, which is in modern-day Israel. Not much is known about his boyhood other than how the elders were very impressed by his wisdom as a boy. His profession, until roughly the age of thirty, was that of a carpenter. At about that age, he became an itinerate preacher, traveling from location to location preaching the word of God. Initially, what set Jesus apart from other preachers of that day was his ability to perform miracles, especially in the area of healing others. People gravitated to him because of his calm and welcoming demeanor. He spoke of God's kingdom after life on this earth had passed. He made an appeal to all people, both rich and poor, to come follow him on his journey back to God. He taught about how we should treat others with love, kindness, and compassion, and that the best barometer was simply to treat others the way we want to be treated. He spoke of God's immeasurable love for us, and that by living our lives in a way that is pleasing to God, we will one day join him in heaven. He emphasized service, humility, forgiveness, and that God's love for us never ends. He taught that even if we turn away from this love, it will pursue us through eternity. His sermons gave hope to all—the poor, the sick, and the downtrodden, as well as the wealthy. He taught that eternal peace and happiness awaited those who followed him toward God.

As Jesus became better known, and as people began following him and flocking to listen to him speak and teach, he was perceived as a threat and a menace by the religious leaders of that day. Being flocked by many, he entered Jerusalem during the Passover festival. Many of his followers hailed him as a miracle worker, the "Son of God," and "King of the Jews." The Jewish high priests and other community leaders immediately felt threatened. As Jesus visited Herod's Temple, he caused a disturbance by overturning the tables of money changers, as the temple was being used for gambling. He was arrested on political charges, which amounted to sedition against the Roman Empire. The high priests allowed Jesus to be transferred into Roman custody so that they would not have to deal with his popularity with his followers. After going through the mockery of a public trial, he was sentenced to death.

Before we can fully appreciate the life, love, and sacrifice of Jesus, we must first have a better understanding of the process of his death. He was sentenced to die by way of Roman crucifixion. This process began by stripping him and tying him to a post in a public location. Next, he was severely flogged. By Jewish law, he was to receive forty lashes across his back by a 'Cat-o'-nine-tails,' which was a leather whip with nine strands at the end. What made this Roman scourging so terrible was that they tied pieces of barbed metal or sharp pieces of bone to the end of each strand. With each lash, the strands wrapped around the body, and the barbs hooked into flesh. The flogger then raked the barbs across the body, causing flesh to rip open, which was followed by profuse bleeding. Not only were bones exposed, but sometimes internal organs, as well. The purpose of this severe beating was to create excruciating pain, as well as profuse bleeding to speed up the death process.

The Gospels tell us that after receiving this scourging, Jesus had to carry the cross through the jeering crowds and up a hill where he would be crucified. A crown of thorns was jammed down onto his head, causing further pain and bleeding. On the hill, the Roman soldiers laid Jesus down onto the crossbar and then drove spikes through his wrists into the wood. Researchers say that the spikes were driven through the wrists so that the spikes would catch on the bones of his wrists and hands. If they had been driven through his hands, they would have just ripped through the flesh between his finger bones. The wrists would allow the spikes to support a man's weight. Attached to the post, down by his feet, was a small platform, angled downward, to which his feet were spiked. The severe beating, the crown of thorns, and being spiked to the cross were all cruel enough, but the real torture was yet to come. As Jesus was hung upright on the cross, there was an immediate struggle to breathe. Because of the position of his arms, his hanging body weight created tremendous pressure on his chest cavity, making every breath difficult. The only way he could fill his lungs with air was to straighten his legs to take the pressure off his chest. Each time he stood, however, he faced the excruciating pain of having his feet spiked to the angled platform. This was the cruel irony of the process. There was an ongoing tradeoff between excruciating pain and not being able to breathe. Oftentimes, if the person was not dying fast enough, the Roman soldiers broke the person's legs below the knee with a club to speed up the process. Throughout his arrest, bogus trial, scourging, humiliation, and crucifixion, Jesus never cursed his tormentors or put up any resistance. To the contrary, as his imminent death was approaching, he actually asked God to forgive his torturers, stating, "Forgive them, Father, for they know not what they do." Ultimately for Jesus, fatigue set in. When he could not stand up any longer, he took his last breath and passed from this earth. It is hard for me to imagine a more cruel or torturous death.

Enduring a different yet also very painful torment were his parents. The Gospels tell of Jesus exchanging glances with his mother as he was carrying the cross and of Jesus speaking to her shortly before he died. As a parent, I cannot imagine the heartache of watching my child go through the worst suffering imaginable as I was forced to stand by helplessly. Somehow, she must have understood that it was part of his earthly destiny. I wonder if she realized, thirty-some years earlier, that the son that she had just delivered into this world would someday deliver her from this world? Even with this knowledge, I can't imagine that it would have made watching her precious son's crucifixion any easier as his mother. I have no doubt—like most parents—that she would have traded places with him at any time.

Earlier in this chapter, I stated that at the core of the Christian faith was the bravest, strongest, and toughest man who ever lived. Here is why I would say such a thing. Over the years, many people have been tortured and killed for their beliefs. The difference is that, at any point during this process, Jesus could have stopped it! He was the Son of God! He had worked miracles and saved the lives of others. Certainly, then, when the going got tough and pain started to become excruciating, he could have called on his Father and saved his own life. *But he chose not to!* He had spent his whole life helping others, healing, uplifting the poor, and teaching people how to treat each other and how to love God. He had touched countless lives, devoting himself to bringing others closer to heaven. He had certainly not done anything to deserve a death penalty! In the end, he endured the worst torture possible without complaining, and he surrendered his life because of his love for me … and you.

This kind of unconditional love for me, in spite of all my faults and all of the bad things I have done in my life, is mind boggling. In my adult life, as I have reflected on the depth of his love, it has helped me to better put things in perspective. I now appreciate more fully the life, death, and resurrection of Jesus. I now realize that God sent us the perfect male role model two thousand years ago. I believe that Jesus was sent to teach us how to live our lives, how to treat other people, and above all else, how to love and serve God. I now know that he truly was a real man's man! As I try each week to live my life more like Jesus, I realize that I still have a lot of work to do and a long way to go before becoming the man I hope to be. However, by trying to follow his example, I know that I have become a better husband, father, son, sibling, teacher, coach, and role model.

Reflecting on the strength of Jesus helps me to put other things in my life in perspective. When I consider the scourging, the minor aches and pains I feel each morning as I get out of bed don't seem as bad. When I think of people shouting and spitting on Jesus and thrusting the crown of thorns on his head as he was carrying the cross for their sins, it makes me think about how I should respond to others when they say something I don't like or agree with. When I reflect on the incredible suffering he endured for me while hanging on the cross, I feel deeply indebted. I now tend to think of and pray for others more often, and I think of what I might be able to do for those in need. I also find myself being more generous to those I don't know through charitable giving. As a further reflection on the strength of Jesus, this past fall, I asked our team to contemplate the life and death of Jesus. I told them that I thought he would have been a *great* football player! Even though he was a peaceful man, I have no doubt that he would have taken God with him on every play. Certainly, he would have worked hard, been a great leader, and would have done anything within the rules to help his teammates succeed. No doubt, he would have felt an obligation to make the most of his talents, and he would have played every play in a way that would make his Father proud. Jesus was the ultimate warrior, as he was tortured and gave his life for his "team." There has never been a better example of courage, selflessness, or loyalty. In short, he would certainly be a guy I would want in my huddle on game night!

In 1926, Dr. James Allen Francis wrote a book entitled "The Real Jesus and Other Sermons." In the last chapter he wrote about the lasting impression Jesus has had on mankind. Over the years different versions of this piece have been published, usually entitled "One Solitary Life" and often times identified as

"Author Unknown." I will share one of the more common versions.

One Solitary Life

He was born in an obscure village, the child of a peasant woman. He grew up in another obscure village, where he worked in a carpenter shop until he was thirty. For three years he was an itinerant preacher. He never wrote a book. He never held an office. He never had a family or owned a house. He didn't go to college. He never traveled more than two hundred miles from the place he was born. He did none of the things usually associated with greatness. He had no credentials but himself. He was only thirty three when public opinion turned against him. His friends deserted him. He was turned over to his enemies and went through the mockery of a trial. He was nailed to a cross between two thieves. While he was dying, his executioners gambled for his clothing, the only property he had on earth. When he was dead, he was laid in a borrowed grave. Twenty centuries have come and gone, and today he is the central figure of much of the human race and the leader of mankind's progress. All the armies that ever marched, all the navies that ever sailed, all the parliaments that ever sat, all the kings that ever reigned, put together, have not affected the life of mankind on earth as much as that One Solitary Life.

I have always appreciated the message delivered by this piece. It emphasizes that during most of Jesus' time on earth, he lived an ordinary life. It is remarkable that despite his humble background, over the past two thousand years no individual, group of people, or world event have shaped mankind as much as the life, death, and enduring life lessons taught by Jesus. In every sense of the word, he truly was a real man's man!

As I mentioned earlier, as Americans, we have the choice about whether we believe in God, Jesus and heaven. Although this decision is mostly something I feel in my heart, there is also a pragmatic side to it. I have always considered myself to be a pretty logical person (although I'm sure there are some who have witnessed my play calling on Friday nights who might question this!). A simple yet logical and somewhat philosophical way of explaining why I choose to believe in God can be broken down into three parts:

> If I live my life on earth as if there is no such thing as God or heaven—and then at the hour of my death realize that they do exist—what will eternity have in store for me?

> If I live my life as if God and heaven do exist—and find out at the hour of my death that there are no such things—at least I will have lived a good life and will have helped to make the world a better place.

> If I believe in God and heaven, choose to live my life accordingly, and ultimately find out that they do exist, I will have lived my life on this earth with a purpose and will be rewarded with eternal peace and happiness. What better reason could there be to believe?

I have learned that when I live each day with my faith at the core, my life seems to have more purpose, and everything begins to make sense. In chapter 4, I mentioned that in high school, being an athlete gave me a sense of identity. As an adult, it is my faith that gives me a sense of identity and purpose—and consequently a sense of fulfillment. Just like all areas of our lives, maintaining a faith relationship with God requires work. As in all relationships, communication is the key. This communication with God takes place in the form of prayer. I usually try to pray when I am alone and quiet so that I can give my undivided attention to God. As I pray in solitude, I often feel a warm, tingling sensation run up my spine. I have always believed that this is the Holy Spirit entering my body.

About a year ago, I learned a new way to pray that I would like to share with you. I have two older brothers, Sam and Kim. As we were growing up, being the youngest boy meant that I was usually the one with the most knots on my head. As they are seven and five years older than I, they were both quite adept at whuppin' me with some regularity, keeping a steady supply of those knots on my noggin. In spite of this, I have always looked up to and admired my older brothers. They have been good male role models for me in my adult life. Sam lives in Florida, and Kim lives in Virginia. We, along with our five sisters, all get to spend a week together each summer.

Last year, I was telling Kim that I was thinking about writing this book, and I asked if he had any suggestions on how to be a better man. His biggest advice revolved around praying for others. He explained that he keeps a prayer list with names of those he thinks are in need of prayer. Almost every day, he will take a few minutes to grab the list and begin to work his way down the page, saying a prayer for each person. As he gets to each new name, he will actually place his finger on the name as he sends up a prayer for that person. He said this makes him feel more of a connection with each person he is praying for, as well as a daily connection with God. He said that by the end of the year, his list is quite long. A few months ago, I started my own prayer list. I started with family, loved ones, and friends. As time has passed, I have added numerous names. I make sure that whenever I tell someone that I will pray for them, I put his or her name on the list so I don't forget. Like my brother, I touch the name as I pray for that person, and I can immediately feel a connection with the person I am praying for. If you feel at times like you are disconnected from God or others in your life, I strongly recommend creating a prayer list to work from. In just a few minutes each day, you can re-establish a connection with the people who are most important in your life, as well as a stronger connection to God. These are both good things!

In summary, all of us will die one day. What matters most is how we choose to live our lives between now and then. God sent us the perfect male role model in Jesus to steer us along the right path. Quite frankly, our faiths are the single-most important things about us. Our faith will determine the course our lives take, faith will affect how we treat others, and faith will influence all of our major decisions as well as where we ultimately will spend eternity. This is not something I am willing to take chances with ... are you?

Overtime

The story is told of an atheist named John who really enjoyed hiking. One day, as he was deep into the woods, he looked up and saw a large and rather hungry-looking grizzly bear staring right at him just a few feet down the path. The man quickly turned to run, but in no time, the grizzly had caught up and knocked him to the ground. As the bear pounced on top of him and raised his huge paw, preparing to strike the death blow, the atheist cried out in fear, "Dear God, please save me!"

Suddenly, the bear's paw froze in midair, the birds stopped chirping, the stream nearby stopped flowing, and an intense sunbeam came down from the sky. A booming voice came from the beam and said, "Well, John, for all these years, you have denied that I exist, yet in your moment of need, you cry out asking me to save you. Does this mean that you now are confessing that I exist and that you actually need me in your life?"

John was a stubborn and very proud man, yet at the same time, he was pretty crafty. So he replied to God, "Well, you know, it does seem to be a little hypocritical. So instead of making me profess to being a Christian, why don't you instead make this bear a Christian?"

So God immediately replied, "Consider it done!"

John smiled smugly. Suddenly, the sunbeam disappeared, the birds started chirping, the stream started flowing again, and the bear very slowly and reverently brought his huge paws together in front of him to get ready to pray. Then the bear reverently prayed, "Dear Lord, thank you for delivering me this meal I'm about to consume!"

Unlike the poor atheist in this story, I am proud of my Christian faith. Like the grizzly, I feel it is important to pray and express words of thanks for the many blessings in my life. As we bring this chapter to a close, I would like to finish with a prayer. I would be quite honored if you would join me:

> "Dear Heavenly Father, thank you for the countless blessings in our lives. Thank you for our wonderful family and friends. Thank you for the ability to see, hear, share, and laugh with those we love. Thank you for the things we often take for granted—a warm house, food on the table, a bed to sleep in, and a place to call home. Please be with those who don't have these things and help them to find joy in their hearts and peace in you. Please be with those who are suffering from illness or disease. May you place your healing hand on them so that they might return to good health. Protect the men and women who serve so proudly in the armed forces to protect our great nation. Help them to realize that their sacrifices are appreciated. Please bring them all home safely. Finally, Lord, please be with us daily on our journeys back to you. Grant us the wisdom, strength, and courage to follow the example set by Jesus so that we may live each day in a way that is pleasing to you. Help us each day to strive to be real men in your eyes, because yours are the ones that count. All these things we ask in your name. Amen."

Thanks for joining with me. I think that was the perfect way to end chapter 6. In the next chapter, we will take a look at where we are hopefully heading as real men. Let's move forward, shall we?

CHAPTER 7

How Far Is Heaven?

WHAT AND WHERE is heaven? This question has been pondered by mankind for thousands of years. Different faith backgrounds have a variety of definitions and descriptions of what heaven must be like. Likewise, our perspectives of heaven often evolve as we grow and mature. I have always been a big fan of ice cream in just about any flavor. I remember as a child believing that heaven must be a place where a person could have as much ice cream as he wanted, anytime he pleased. At my current stage in life, however, I would have to add the stipulation that, in heaven, I could eat as much ice cream as I wanted without gaining weight. Some things do change as we get older.

Perhaps unlimited amounts of ice cream *are* available in heaven. *Webster's Dictionary* defines heaven as "A state or place of complete happiness or perfect rest, attained by the good after death." I think most faiths believe that heaven is a wonderful place that our souls pass on to as our earthly lives come to an end. Most Christian denominations also espouse that our ability to attain eternal peace and happiness with God in heaven depends on how we live our lives during our time on earth. Being raised in the Christian faith, it is this concept that leads me to believe that heaven really is not that far away!

The story is told of a holy man who asked God to show him the difference between heaven and hell. God agreed to do so and took him down a long hallway. At the end of the hallway were two closed doors. God opened the first door and told the man to look inside. The man immediately noticed a wonderful smell wafting through the door. As he peered inside, he saw a large table with a huge pot of delicious-smelling stew. Seated around the table were many people, each with a haggard, hopeless, and emaciated appearance. The man asked God how all of these people could be starving as they sat around a huge pot of delicious stew. God answered, "Watch and see." The man soon noticed that each person was equipped with a long-handled spoon—and that each handle was slightly longer than the arm of the person who held it. Each time the people dipped their spoons into the pot and tried to feed themselves, they would barely miss their mouths because the handle was too long, and the food would be spilled and wasted. After a few moments of this, God said, "My friend, you have just seen a glimpse of hell!" God then shut the first door and opened the second. Once again, the same wonderful smell of stew wafted through the door. As the man looked inside, he immediately noticed that there was another large table with a huge pot of stew with many people seated around it. Each person was equipped with the same long-handled spoon he had seen behind the first door, but every person in this room appeared to be well fed, healthy, and happy. He watched as everyone dipped into the pot and then reached with their long-handled spoons to feed the person seated across from them. After a few moments, God said, "My son, you have just seen a glimpse of heaven!"

I think this story certainly relates to our time on earth. If we are only concerned with taking care of ourselves, or "feeding only ourselves" as in the story, we are doomed to live a shallow and unfulfilling existence. I do believe that those who find themselves living in their own private hell are usually mired down into a state of self-pity and selfish behavior. It is through "feeding others" and devoting our time and energy to helping those around us that we share glimpses of heaven by the way we choose to live our lives. In so many ways, we have the ability to bring "pieces of heaven" to others during our time on earth.

It is through my family and loved ones that I most frequently give and receive these glimpses of heaven. My blessings center around my beautiful wife and our four precious children. As a young man, I used to dream that one day I would meet someone with whom I would fall in love. In return, that person's love for me would make my life complete. That dream came true. Frankly, the love and devotion I have for Jackie is a choice I make each day. By making sure she knows that she is still beautiful to me and that I love her more deeply now than ever before, I can bring glimpses of heaven into her life. I'm sure that in heaven, wives know that their husbands love them, and they are told frequently how beautiful they are. I believe Jackie deserves these same things during her time on earth, as well! Why wait?

I mentioned in chapter 3 that a big part of my vocation as a father is to convince my children each day that I love them. Even more than the verbal communication, I hope my actions bring glimpses of heaven into their lives. Likewise, I receive so many blessings through my interactions with my children. Knowing that Luke, even as a college student, still loves to spend time with his dad makes my heart happy. Hanging out with Luke and Cal and just making one another laugh about the silliest things brings much sunshine into my life. Seeing Abby smile when I tell her that she's beautiful makes me smile, as well. Not long ago, I found a note that Meggie had put on my day planner that I take to school each day that read, "Daddy, I love you soooo much with all my heart." Finding this note made me happy for the rest of the day. I have no doubt that fathers in heaven receive notes frequently from their children that say, "Daddy, I love you soooo much," with several o's after the s. Certainly, I receive daily glimpses of heaven through my children. I can only pray that they might receive that same gift from me.

As I stated in an earlier chapter, my parents raised me in a Christian household where I knew every day that I was loved and considered a gift from God. I have no doubt that in heaven, every person feels loved and cherished. My parents gave me daily glimpses of heaven by the way they raised our family, and for this I am forever grateful. With four children of my own now, it is my turn to pass on this legacy.

I also stated earlier that part of my vocation as a husband and father is that I need to be a spiritual leader in my household. I want to be a pillar of strength, faith, and hope for my family. Through my actions, I want my children to see that it is important each day to thank God for the countless ways our lives have been blessed. Each night before we eat supper, we join hands and say the Bless Us, O Lord pre-meal prayer. We then each thank God for blessings in our lives and then add a petition of prayer for someone or something we think is in need of God's help. By doing this every night before we eat, I hope we are instilling the importance of daily prayer in our children. I want them to learn that our faith can be an incredible source of strength, both in good times and bad, as we live our daily lives. I want them to understand that Jesus was sent to us to be an example of Christian behavior. I also want them to realize the depth of his love for each of us as he suffered and died on the cross. Ultimately, I want them to appreciate the significance of his resurrection and ascension into heaven. As their father, if I can help each of them understand these concepts a little better, I am truly providing them glimpses of heaven.

In my role as a teacher and coach, I also have an opportunity to bring pieces of heaven to the young people I work with each day. By teaching and encouraging them to pray on a daily basis, I am helping strengthen their faith relationships with God. Part of my job is to instill discipline and an appreciation for hard work into their daily routines. Hopefully, they will begin to understand that the best way they can thank their parents and honor God for the many gifts they have been given is to give everything they have and do their very best to become the people God created them to be. In my role as a coach, I am able to teach a code of conduct for manhood. I want all of our players to love and honor their parents and to eventually become faithful husbands to their wives and loving fathers to their children. I want them to realize that their success as men doesn't depend on what they own, but it should be measured instead by their capacity to love and be loved. I want to teach them that there is a purpose for their existence in this world and that God had something very special in mind when He created each of them. As our players witness our coaching staff modeling Christ-like behavior, hopefully they receive glimpses of heaven through us. Through these lessons, in turn, our older players often become solid Christian leaders to the underclassmen, and the legacy continues.

It is our hope that as players graduate and mature into young adults, they will continue on their Christian journey to become men who partake in service to others. Each selfless act of generosity, each kind deed we do for others provides a glimpse into heaven. When we receive these acts of kindness, we are more likely to do something nice for someone else in return. This is how the chain begins, with the end result being that we continually receive glimpses of heaven, and, in return, we pass them on to others.

How far is heaven? Not really very far at all. In a very real sense, it is only as far as our hearts choose for it to be. This is another decision we make each day!

As I've reflected on my journey with God, I have often asked myself, "Where do I find meaning and purpose in my life?" I think it's good to periodically take account of where our priorities lie. Where is our time and energy spent? What "wall of fame" are we striving to have our names etched upon when our lives on earth end? Would it be the Golf Wall of Fame? Or, perhaps, it might be the "top salesman" or "top wage earner" or maybe the hardest worker with the most hours spent. Oftentimes, I question myself about this during football season. To what wall of fame am I dedicating my life?

A few years ago, I was contemplating this thought and wrote the following poem:

Heaven's Wall

As we live our lives on earth
What do we hope to gain?
Is it power that we seek
Or is it wealth or fame?

Are we busy building up
Possessions here on earth?
Do we use the things we own
To measure our true worth?

Or are we more concerned with how
We treat our fellow man
Knowing that the Golden Rule
Follows God's master plan?

And if we choose to steer our lives
Along Christ Jesus' path
He will be the author of
Our celestial epitaph.

So when we stand at heaven's gates
We'll look and find our name
Shining brightly and inscribed
On heaven's wall of fame.

I believe that there will come a day when I will be held accountable for the gifts God has given me, how I chose to use those gifts, and, ultimately, the influence I had on others. I want to live my life with purpose; I want my journey to matter. I want to make a difference for those whose lives I touch. I do want to make it to heaven, and, along the way, I want to bring as many people with me as I can.

I pray that if I work hard, do my best to live my life according to the example set by Jesus, and, in the process, strive to get others to do the same, I might someday find my name etched in a place of honor on heaven's wall of fame. I now realize that this is the wall I am seeking.

When my time on earth is finished, my hope is to hear God say, "Job well done, my good and faithful servant." I can only imagine the pride, joy, and honor that will fill my heart. I will know I have completed my last contest and have won the ultimate championship. I will have claimed victory in the game of life.

Overtime

What if we were suddenly informed that this was to be our last day on this earth? I would assume most of us would feel an intense urge to make the most of every minute of the day. We would probably make a profound effort to spend as much quality time with our family and loved ones as we could in the few hours that remained. We would probably find ourselves saying things to the people we love that we might not normally say. We would certainly want our loved ones to know how we feel about them. When put in this perspective, it probably makes us wonder why we don't do a better job of spending quality time and sharing how we really feel with our loved ones more frequently. We never really know for sure when our moment of "departure" from this world will occur!

Similarly, as our time of death was approaching, we would probably ask ourselves a few questions: "Have I lived a good life? Does my family truly know how much I love them? Is God proud of the way I have conducted myself and made use of the gifts he gave me? Have I done what I needed to do during my time on earth to deserve to be admitted into heaven? Do I really deserve to go to heaven?" These are all questions that would probably cross our minds somewhere toward the end. How would you answer each of these questions at this point in your life?

A little lighter way to ponder this is related in the following silly story.

> When Forrest Gump arrived at the Pearly Gates, seeking admission into heaven, he was greeted by St. Peter. The wise saint told Forrest that, before he could be admitted into heaven, he would first have to answer three questions. The first question St. Peter asked Forrest was, "How many days of the week start with the letter *T*, and what are they?"
>
> Forrest replied, in his slow, southern drawl, "Well, that is easy. There are two—today and tomorrow!" There was a little bit of a line behind Forrest, and the people in it began to chuckle at his answer.
>
> St. Peter, being slightly irritated by this, decided that he was going to make the second question harder than usual. For question two, he asked, "How many seconds are there in a year?"
>
> Forrest thought for a few seconds and then said, "Well, that's easy, too—there are twelve!"
>
> Now St. Peter even began to chuckle, and he asked, "How in the world did you come up with that?"
>
> Forrest replied, "Well, there's January second, February second, March second ..."
>
> At this, the crowd really began to laugh out loud. St. Peter was now visibly irritated, so he decided to prove a point to the others by asking an impossibly difficult third question. St. Peter then asked, "OK, Forrest, for your third question, tell me—what is God's first name?" Now, St. Peter smiled smugly as he watched Forrest scratch his head.
>
> Suddenly, Forrest's face lit up as he said, "I know! His name is Andy!"

Holding back hearty laughter, St. Peter asked, "Well, now, tell me … where did you come up with a name like that?"

Forrest, with a huge smile on his face, broke into song, "Andy walks with me, Andy talks with me, Andy tells me I am his own!"

St. Peter, being on the verge of saying something not fit for angels, quickly opened the gates to heaven and said, *"Run, Forrest! Run!"*

I am pretty confident we will not be asked these same three questions as we await admission into heaven. However, it is possible that different questions might have to be answered in regard to our accountability for the way we lived our lives on earth. What if we are asked about what we did with the gifts God gave us throughout our lifetimes? What if we are asked about the kind of influence we chose to be on others, those whose lives we touched each day? What if we are asked about how hard we worked to follow Jesus' example in our daily lives? What if we are questioned about the degree to which we allowed our faith in God to guide us each day? If we one day are judged on these principles, where will we stand?

I believe the better job we do of bringing glimpses of heaven to others during our time on earth, the closer we are to entering God's kingdom when our last day on earth is complete. As stated in the last chapter, Jesus laid the groundwork in showing us how this is done. As real men, if we commit ourselves to living our lives each day in a way that is pleasing to God, perhaps one day we will meet each other inside those Pearly Gates as we proudly see our names inscribed on heaven's wall! What a wonderful day that will be!

CHAPTER 8

The Keys to Happiness

"MOST MEN LEAD lives of quiet desperation." Henry David Thoreau wrote these words 150 years ago as he reflected on the void that exists in most men's hearts during their time on earth. For many men, these words still hold true today. Why do so many men feel this void or this desperation in their lives? Obviously, something is missing or out of place. I would like for us to spend this chapter discussing several concepts that can help lead to a happier and more fulfilling life. None of these are impossible tasks, and they can certainly add meaning to our existence.

Over the years as I have spoken at coaching clinics or other venues, I have been asked, "What are the keys to success?" By and large, I think these can be broken down into two categories. The first is what I call the "mechanics of success." These are the physical activities to get you where you want to be, including working hard, being loyal and dependable for others, and setting goals to serve as a road map for achievement. Although these are all important to attain success, I believe the second category, which tends to be more philosophical, leads to greater accomplishments and certainly a more fulfilling life.

I don't believe that being successful necessarily equates to wealth or social status. Our time on earth should not be like a Monopoly game, where our main objective is to ultimately take over as many possessions as we can to be declared "winners" by game's end. Truth is, one day the game of life will end for us all. At that point, what meaning will all of our earthly goods possess, since we can't take them with us? Ironically, I think everyone knows people who are wealthy and have many material possessions but are really unhappy in their personal lives. Interestingly, studies have shown that suicide rates are highest around the world in wealthy countries and occur most commonly in families of reasonable affluence. Being wealthy has little to do with contentment or joy. Therefore, it must not be the key to success. There is a saying that seems quite appropriate: "Success is not the key to happiness. Happiness is the key to success!"

In this philosophical approach toward happiness, we must first take stock of ourselves and our relationships with others. How do we treat those whose lives we come in contact with each day? I believe our actions have a mirror effect—meaning that the image we present to others will usually be reflected right back at us. Likewise, the words we choose to use with others have the same result as shouting into a cave—good or bad, they will come echoing right back at us. It very simply ties in with the Golden Rule; treat others as we want to be treated. I have grown to believe that this is a fundamental weakness that has developed in our society today. It is so easy to point the finger of blame at others for our lot in life. Yet, we often fail to recognize that we are primarily responsible for our own happiness.

Consider for a moment that over half of all marriages in America end in divorce. Then consider that in many parts of provincial China, it is customary for a man and woman who are considering divorce to stand in front of a committee to publicly share the problems their marriage is facing. However, before either of them can say anything negative against his or her spouse, he or she must first spend twenty minutes discussing his or her own faults, shortcomings, personality flaws, and ways that he or she has contributed to the dissolution of the marriage. Needless to say, the Chinese experience only a fraction of the divorces we have in this country. I believe our society would be well served to have this kind of self-examination and personal accountability. I also contend that an honest and thorough self-assessment is the first step in leading to a happier, more fulfilled life.

The second step toward happiness is to periodically take a few moments to realize the many blessings we all have in our lives. I am reminded of "the World's Funniest Joke." At the start of the twenty-first century, thousands of people around the world were polled to determine what joke would be deemed most humorous. The following was the favorite:

> Sherlock Holmes and his trusty assistant, Dr. Watson, were on a camping trip. In the middle of the night, Sherlock awoke and immediately took notice of the billions of brightly lit stars in the sky. He nudged his friend, who was sound asleep, and said, "Watson, I want you to look up at all the stars in the sky and tell me what you deduce from what you see."

> Watson, who was well aware of his friend's uncanny ability to trick him with these types of questions, was determined not to let it happen again. After pondering for a few moments, he replied, "Well, Sherlock, I recall from my background in astronomy that all of those stars in the sky are actually suns—very much like our own. As such, it is highly likely that many of them have planets revolving around them, as in our own solar system. Consequently, I would deduce that, somewhere in the universe, there is a planet very similar to Earth, and that there is, indeed, life elsewhere in the universe."

Watson was confident that he'd nailed it. With a smug look on his face, he asked, "Well, Sherlock, how did I do?"

Sherlock replied, with a rather disgusted tone to his voice, "Well, Watson, you nitwit! You were supposed to deduce that someone has stolen our tent!"

Although I know I've laughed harder at other jokes over the years, I think there's an important message we can take from poor Dr. Watson's ill-fated deduction. How many times in our lives do we fail to see what is right in front of us because we are so intent on gazing at the stars beyond? How often do we take our families and loved ones for granted while we are in pursuit of a higher salary, a new car, or a bigger home?

An interesting perspective on this is to imagine how desperate you would immediately become if you were suddenly approached on the street by someone who took your keys and wallet away. Imagine how you would feel if you were told you would never see your family, your home, or your vehicle again, and that you were destined to live the rest of your life on the street with none of these comforts. After two weeks on the street, imagine how ecstatic you would be if that same person gave back your keys and wallet and said that your family and friends were waiting at home for your arrival, and your life was going to return to normal. I'm sure this exercise would help each of us realize just how blessed we truly are! The process of realizing and being thankful for our many blessings is the second step toward happiness and success in life. If we ever begin to doubt how blessed we are, we should simply make a list of everything we are thankful for. List every person we care about, every skill we possess, everything we own, every blessing we have ever received. Try this just once, and we'll see that we have far more blessings than we originally could have imagined. However far we get on this list, make an effort to express gratitude for each one. Being grateful for our countless blessings is one of the most important steps we can take toward happiness!

In addition to taking an honest account of ourselves and realizing the countless ways our lives have been blessed, the third key to success is to find happiness and contentment by living our lives with purpose. Thoreau's words "most men lead lives of quiet desperation" have never rung more true than they do today. So many people, both male and female, go through their lives lacking a real sense of purpose. Consequently, their existence seems to lack meaning.

Recently, I read an article about the top ten things that lead to happiness in a person's job. The results were interesting. The number-one item was not salary, benefits, or a new company car. Surprisingly, the top factor was having a job where workers felt they were helping others. Reading this made me smile, and it also helped me understand why I love my job as a teacher and coach. I am a firm believer in the phrase "We are God's hands." When we do things for other people, they see God through us. Ultimately, this adds value and meaning to our lives, and it can be an ongoing source of gratification and happiness. When we work in service for others, our lives become filled with purpose. Living a purposeful life ultimately leads to fulfillment and happiness!

There are a couple of sayings I've always liked that seem appropriate here. "Preach the gospel at all times. When necessary, use words." The other is "We may be the only Bible some people ever read." I hope the young people I come in contact with at Roncalli see Christ through my actions each day. Oftentimes, I see Christ through them! This is truly what makes Roncalli such a special place and leads to great job satisfaction for me.

I realize that many careers are not as conducive to helping others as is teaching. However, regardless of a person's career, individuals can always find ways of helping others—through volunteer work and generosity. I believe helping others is a huge step toward happiness and ultimate success in life.

The fourth key to success is realizing that our lives are filled with choices. Each day, we must choose our attitudes, because this truly is one of the few things in life over which we have complete control. Winston Churchill once said, "A pessimist sees the difficulty in every opportunity; an optimist sees the opportunity in every difficulty." We get to choose each day which of these two philosophies we will adopt. We must also decide how we are going to treat those around us and how we are going to respond to the way others treat us. Each day, we choose who to love and who to separate from that love. And finally, we choose whether or not we are going to be happy. Without question, happiness is a choice! There is an old saying, "Pain is inevitable, suffering is optional." Adversity is a given, we will face it the rest of our lives. However, the attitude we keep and how we choose to deal with hardships is entirely up to us each day. This is also a true sign of our character. Eleanor Roosevelt once said, "No one can make you feel inferior without your consent." I contend that no one can make us unhappy without our consent. Being happy is ultimately a choice we must make before it can become reality.

As we control our attitudes, we also take control of our integrity and character. Interestingly, the qualities that define character—work ethic, honesty, kindness, loyalty, dependability, and so on—are all traits over which we have control. We do not need extraordinary mental or physical talents to possess character. Our personalities are what other people usually see in us. Character is what God sees and what we see in ourselves. Our daily attitudes, which we do have complete control over, are the foundations of our characters. As we choose to maintain great attitudes and live our lives with character, our self-esteem elevates, which ultimately increases happiness.

Just like we remind our players before they leave the locker room before a game, the fifth and final key to success is to "take

God with you on every play." This, too, is our choice. We decide every day whether or not we pray, and, likewise, we choose to what degree we allow God into our hearts to guide us. Clinical studies have proven the merits of prayer. Researchers have found that regular prayer helps reduce anxiety and depression and also works to boost self-esteem. Studies have also shown that people who pray regularly tend to lead happier lives and that married couples who incorporate prayer into their relationships tend to have happier and longer-lasting marriages. Each year, people around the world spend billions of dollars on medications and treatments to deal with anxiety, depression, and self-esteem issues. Prayer is free, and we can do it any time we please, as much as we like! Additionally, prayer is not harmful to others or to ourselves, even in large doses. Quite to the contrary!

I firmly believe that faith and prayer are at the core of true happiness! As I reflect on the stages of my life when I allowed myself to grow distant from God, without question, those were the times when I felt a void in my heart and a lack of purpose in my life. I firmly believe that this is the void that results in many men "leading lives of quiet desperation" that Mr. Thoreau wrote about many years ago.

As I have learned to fill that void with God's love, every aspect of my life becomes more fulfilling—personally, professionally, and spiritually. As I follow the advice we give our players before every game, and I "take God with me on every play," happiness seems to follow. Whether we are dealing with issues at work, struggling in a relationship, or battling with various setbacks in life, taking God with us in everything we do will make problems more manageable. Maintaining strong faith relationships with God will also add meaning and purpose to our lives and help us to be more grateful for the gifts with which we've been blessed. This is the ultimate key to happiness!

Overtime

There is a legend about a man who lived in a kingdom far away. Because he had been raised poor, had lived a hard life, and had not had many things go his way, he was an angry man. As he became an adult, his anger showed in his appearance. His face had become gnarled and disfigured, a reflection of his surly attitude.

One day, the king sent word across the kingdom that his beautiful daughter, the princess, was of age to be married. Being a loving father, he wanted her to choose her own husband. Thus, he extended an invitation to all unmarried men in the kingdom to go through an interview process, and then the top-five candidates would each spend one day with his daughter. From these brief courtships, she would select her husband.

Although the man's face was gnarled, he was a very intelligent fellow. He knew this could be an opportunity to change his lot in life. Yet, he also knew that the princess was the most beautiful woman in the kingdom, and stories were told that she was just as beautiful on the inside. How could she ever fall in love with someone like him?

There was a wizard in a province nearby who the man had met a few years earlier. The man took his life savings and went to see the wizard. He asked if the wizard could make him a beautiful mask, one that could not be detected. The wizard said that he could, but there was one stipulation. The mask would be undetectable for one year; however, after exactly one year, the mask would fall off. The man decided that it was worth a shot, that potentially one year of happiness was better than none. After paying the wizard, the man received a very handsome new face.

The man was crafty enough to make it into the top five. When his day of courtship with the princess came to pass, he used his intelligence to present himself as a kind, gentle, charming, and caring man. Much to his delight, when the whole courtship process was over, the beautiful princess chose him to be her husband. They soon had a wonderful wedding, which was easily the happiest day of his life. On their wedding day, his new bride shared with him that he was her choice not because of his handsome looks, but because of the wonderful person he was on the inside. This made him very happy, yet he knew that he was living a lie. He also knew that he had only a year to live this dream life he had created for himself.

He soon found that the princess truly was just as beautiful on the inside as her appearance on the outside. He quickly fell deeply in love with her. With the knowledge that he only had one year to spend with her, he dedicated his life to being the best husband he could be for her. He treated her each day with love, respect, kindness, and devotion. She often told him that he made her happier than she had ever been before, which in turn made his heart happy. Although he knew he only had a few months to be a part of her life, he was committed to make her life joyous and fulfilled during that time.

When the one year date arrived, the man knew that he had to tell her the truth. He reluctantly began by saying, "My dear wife, there is something I need to show you." At this point, he began to peel the handsome mask from his face. His wife looked on in disbelief. As he stood there with the mask in his hands, she just looked at him with a confused expression on her face.

Finally, she said, "I don't understand. Why would you be wearing a mask that looks exactly like your face?" Startled, the man quickly looked in the mirror. To his disbelief, his face actually looked exactly like the handsome mask he had been wearing. He suddenly realized that he had actually become the handsome prince that he had chosen to be during his one year of marriage. Legend has it that they lived happily ever after.

So it is with life. We have the choice each day to decide who we want to be, how we are going to treat others, and ultimately how we are going to live our lives. I believe that we all have seeds of good and seeds of evil inside our hearts. The seeds that grow and take over are the ones that are nurtured. This is a choice we make each day. Over time, we will actually become the traits we display in our daily lives. This becomes our character and who we really are. Which seeds are we going to choose to nourish? I humbly realize that I need God's help with this. When I invite him into my heart each day, He takes care of this nurturing process. He always makes the right choice on which seeds to nourish!

CHAPTER 9

The Challenge

THEY SAY THAT any good speaker should do three basic things when presenting a talk. You should first briefly tell your listeners what you are going to talk about. During your talk, you should discuss the topics you said you were going to talk about. Finally, you should conclude by briefly summarizing what you just talked about. I am going to follow this same pattern in this book. In the foreword, I described the talk that I gave at St. Jude's a couple of summers ago. I mentioned that in this talk, I focused on the four cornerstones of manhood, and I said that this book would be dedicated to discussing each of these in more detail. In chapter 1, we looked at some alarming statistics in America that result from the lack of strong, loving male role models in many households. In chapter 2, we introduced the first cornerstone of manhood by discussing similarities and differences that exist between most men and women. We then used this information to create ideas on how we can become better husbands for our wives. Chapter 3 led us to the second cornerstone—being loving fathers to our children and better understanding our "vocations" as husbands and fathers. In chapter 4, we described the essence of coaching, and that being a "lifetime coach" is far more important than winning games or trophies. In chapter 5, we took a look at the 2002 Roncalli High School state championship football season and emphasized some of the life lessons learned through athletics. Chapter 6 led us to a more detailed look at the life and death of Jesus and the unbelievable influence he has had on mankind. We emphasized that He is the perfect role model for men everywhere. We tied this in with chapter 7, where we pointed out that we have opportunities each day to bring glimpses of heaven to those around us. The more we do this, the more inclined others will be to do the same. This tends to be perpetual, with the end result being that we continually give and receive pieces of heaven. Consequently, heaven is not really that far away. In chapter 8, we discussed the keys to happiness. We emphasized that each of the five keys to happiness are attainable and that ultimately we are all responsible for our daily attitudes and our own happiness.

Finally, this brings us to chapter 9. This is the final chapter, and it will serve primarily as the summary of the book. This chapter will also conclude with a challenge to all who read it. Since this book was written by a man, it contains primarily a man's perspective on most of the concepts addressed. However, it is my hope that many females will read this book as well and will appreciate the primary message presented. If, in fact, you are female and like the message, please consider inviting other women to read the book, as well. Ultimately, I hope you will find it worthy to share with the men in your lives. My hope is that we can get the basic message out to as many men as possible. This primary message is that it is time for us, as men, to step up and become the men God created us to be!

The best way to build the foundation of becoming a real man is to focus on the four cornerstones of manhood. Again, this starts by being good husbands for our wives. I think it is good for us to occasionally remind ourselves of the wedding vows we made in front of our family, friends, and God. We promised on our wedding day to love, respect, and honor our wives. Especially as we have children, we must always remember that the way we conduct ourselves in our marriages creates a legacy for our children and their future relationships. Whether good or bad, our children will be inclined to imitate behavior they have witnessed in their parents' marriage relationship as they later fall in love and get married. How we treat their mothers will set a huge precedent in this regard.

A young man was chatting with his grandfather as their family was celebrating the sixty-fifth wedding anniversary of his grandparents. The young man asked his grandfather what the secret was to his long and successful marriage. His wise grandfather answered, "I was always careful to never criticize your grandmother for her shortcomings or when she did something wrong. I always kept in mind that because of her shortcomings and weaknesses, she could not find a better husband than me!" If we can combine this wisdom with the Chinese practice of not criticizing our spouses until we are first willing to spend twenty minutes publicly declaring our own mistakes, weaknesses, and shortcomings, we will be on our way to a strong and long-lasting marriage!

Once we have fortified the first cornerstone of being a good husband, we can next begin to focus on being a strong and loving father to our children. The decision to be a good father is up to us each day. I recently heard President Barrack Obama state, "Being a good father to my children is the most important job I will ever have in my life." Regardless of our political inclinations, whatever they might be, I thought this was a very profound statement for the president of the United States to make. The work of raising our children and guiding them to become the people God created them to be truly *is* the most important job we have as fathers. This, along with loving their mothers, is one of the strongest traits of real men. As we make our *vocation* of being good husbands and fathers a daily priority, we should often ask ourselves, "Was I the type of man today that my wife and children want me to be?" If we can regularly answer this question affirmatively, we have a good start on creating a strong foundation of manhood.

Being a good role model and positive leader in the community is the third cornerstone of being a real man. I focused earlier in the book on being a "lifetime coach," regardless of what level or team we might be coaching. Anyone who has played sports is aware of the powerful influence coaches have on young people. As coaches, it is good to ask ourselves, "How do I want to be remembered?" Coaching provides daily opportunities to truly make a difference in the hearts, minds, and souls of today's youth. We have a distinct opportunity to nourish the "seeds of good" in their hearts. Far beyond teaching them how to win a game, we can guide them to become champions in the game of life! Next to their parents, we can be the strongest positive influence in their lives. When we do this well, we become heroes in our players' eyes.

Being a "lifetime coach" is not restricted only to athletics. This also pertains to other areas of young people's lives. Wherever our children's interests lie, we can be positive male role models. If their talents are in music or drama, or if they are interested in art or Boy Scouts, we can still be "lifetime coaches" in their lives. Any time we volunteer our time and are able to be present in our children's lives, we are convincing them that we love them and that they are a priority in our lives. As a community volunteer, we can also make a difference in other young lives. As we become good role models and positive leaders in our community, our foundations as real men become stronger.

The fourth cornerstone—striving each day to strengthen our faith relationships with God—is the last pillar we must put into place for our foundation. Our goal should be to "take God with us on every play." Inviting God into our hearts daily will give us a sense of identity and purpose and will consequently add meaning and fulfillment to our lives. As we live each day to bring honor to God, we can feel his presence in everything we do. I have learned over the years that when this fourth cornerstone is strong, the other three become stronger as a result. When I try to live my life in a way that is pleasing to God, I truly want to be a better husband for Jackie and will act accordingly. With faith as my foundation, I am driven to be the best father I can be. I become even more motivated to convince my children that I love them, and this also increases my desire to guide them on their journeys to God. When I take God with me each day, I become more inclined to want to be a good role model and a positive influence on the young people I work with each day. In short, when the cornerstone of my faith is in place, it profoundly affects all of the other important areas of my life in a positive way! This, ultimately, leads to my own personal fulfillment and happiness.

As a Christian, the cornerstone of my faith influences who I am and how I choose to live my life more than any other factor. At the core of my Christian faith is a man who lived two thousand years ago. No person who has walked the face of the earth before or since has influenced others as much as Jesus. Historian Phillip Schaff described this overwhelming impact as he wrote, "This Jesus of Nazareth, without money and arms, conquered more millions than Alexander, Caesar, Mohammed and Napoleon; without science ... he shed more light on things human and divine than all philosophers and scholars combined; without the eloquence of schools, he spoke such words of life as were never spoken before or since, and produced effects which lie beyond the reach of orator or poet; without writing a single line, he set more pens in motion, and furnished themes for more sermons, orations, discussions, learned volumes, works of art, and songs of praise than the whole army of great men of ancient and modern times." With over two billion followers in the world today, Christianity has almost twice as many followers as the next four major world religions combined. Certainly, the enduring and powerful influence of the lessons taught by Jesus is undisputable. What continues to be most inspirational to me, however, is the humanity of Jesus. Far beyond the miracles he performed with physical healing and feeding hundreds with the loaves and fish, his most enduring lessons came from the humility he showed in his acts of love, acceptance, kindness and forgiveness toward others. For centuries, his teachings have provided peace and hope for mankind during our time on earth and in the hereafter. As a man in today's world, it inspires me to know that I, like Jesus, possess the ability to love and accept, as well as to be kind and forgiving of others. We all have the ability to embrace the characteristics displayed by Jesus in the way he treated others. When we choose to live our lives like Jesus in an effort to please God, we can also have a profound influence on the world around us. When we work to change the lives of those around us in a positive way, our lives change in a positive way as a result. This is the beauty of the Christian faith.

An interesting perspective is for each of us to pause and think of the person who has touched our life and influenced us in the most profound way. Envision the person who has lifted us up and inspired us to want to be better people, to treat others with love and respect, and to always give our best to become who we want to be. This person might be a relative, friend, teacher, coach, or mentor. Odds are, they are probably not particularly rich or famous, but because they took a special interest in us, they inspired us to give our best. The point here is that we do not have to be beautiful, brilliant, athletic or wealthy to make a positive influence in the lives of others. We can all achieve this simply by following the example set by Jesus in how we treat other people. In a very real sense, we can influence the world around us in a positive way! This is all part of the cornerstone of striving each day to strengthen our faith and live our lives in a way that is pleasing to God. The better job we do with this, the more fulfilled our lives become!

As we seek happiness in our lives, we must again understand that this is our own responsibility. Accountability starts with us. The following is a famous poem that I think is appropriate and demonstrates this.

"The Man in the Glass"

When you get what you want in your struggle for self
And the world makes you king for a day,
Just go to the mirror and look at yourself,
And see what that man has to say.

For it isn't your father or mother or wife,
Who judgment upon you must pass;
The fellow whose verdict counts most in your life
Is the man staring back from the glass.

He's the fellow to please, never mind all the rest.
For he's with you clear up to the end,
And you've passed your most dangerous, difficult test
If the man in the glass is your friend.

You may be like Jack Horner and "chisel" a plum,
And think you're a wonderful guy,
But the man in the glass says you're only a bum
If you can't look him straight in the eye.

You can fool the whole world down the pathway of years
And get pats on the back as you pass,
But your final reward will be heartache and tears
If you've cheated the man in the glass!

—Dale Wimbrow
1895–1954

Certainly, God is fully aware of our daily attitudes, activities, and conduct. Likewise, so are we! These are choices we make each day. It is impossible to fool ourselves in regard to our own character. The man in the glass doesn't lie. When we look in the mirror, what do we see? Maybe more importantly, do we like what we see? Do we see a man of honesty, character, and integrity? Do we see a guy who gives his best each day to be the man that his wife, children, and God want him to be? Are we proud of the man staring back from the glass?

The good news is that if we answered "no" to any of the above questions, with some work and determination, we can change this answer. It is never too late. The tougher the task is going to be to change, the more we need to be humble enough to ask God for His assistance. With His help, anything is possible! God can be such a strong and powerful force in our lives if only we allow Him to be. Likewise, our faith can provide great hope for the future.

As we age, we tend to look back on our lives when we were at our physical prime, longing for those days to return. In our hearts, we know that they never will. However, as people of faith, we should not look back to our best days. We should look forward to them—they are yet to come! If we follow in Jesus' footsteps, it's very clear that our best days lie before us—days spent in eternal peace and happiness. At my age, I now realize that my top priority in this life is to make it into heaven. My ultimate goal is to bring as many people with me as I can. I would be honored if you would join me! If we commit to living our lives as real men, this wish can become reality. Let's be the spark to get a fire going. My challenge to anyone who reads this book is to join in a movement toward getting as many men as possible across this great nation to step up and become real men! Obviously, it starts with each of us, individually, making the commitment in our own lives. From there, we can inspire others to do the same.

I would like to finish this book with a quote from Nelson Mandela, the courageous and much revered South African leader. He said, "Our deepest fear is not that we are inadequate. Our deepest fear is that we are powerful beyond measure. It is our light, not our darkness, that most frightens us. We ask ourselves, who am I to be brilliant, gorgeous, talented and fabulous? Actually, who are you not to be? You are a child of God. Your playing small doesn't serve the world. There is nothing enlightened about shrinking so that other people won't feel insecure around you. We are born to make manifest the glory of God that is within us. It is not just in some of us, it is in everyone. And as we let our own light shine, we unconsciously give other people permission to do the same. As we are liberated from our own fear, our presence automatically liberates others." In summary, when we liberate ourselves and let our light shine, our presence lights the way for others and encourages them to do the same. If we, as real men, all work together toward this common goal, imagine the difference we can make for the world around us! Come on, fellas, we can do this! Every journey begins with a first step. Let us all begin taking strides toward becoming Real Men. I, for one, believe it is our destiny!

Overtime

As we have spoken a lot in this book about being a positive influence on others, there are two organizations I would like to acknowledge as having an influence on my life both as a high school athlete and as a high school coach. As I was attending Plainfield High School just outside of Indianapolis, Indiana, as a teenager, I really enjoyed being a part of the Fellowship of Christian Athletes organization. We had an FCA "huddle" at Plainfield High School, and I really enjoyed attending FCA camp during the summer. It was a great way for teenagers to enjoy one another's company in Christ-centered activities. It also was a great way to create a solid Christian faith foundation. With FCA chapters all across the country today, this organization continues to be a powerful Christian influence on both athletes and coaches alike. If you are a teacher, coach, or someone who would like to look into getting an FCA chapter started at your school, go to http://www.fca.org for information on how to get started.

In recent years as a coach, a second organization we have worked with is SportsLeader. This is an organization designed to help both coaches and athletes develop stronger virtues and character. Lou Judd is the director of SportsLeader, and he has done a great job of working with coaches on how to develop boys into virtuous men. He has helped me—as well as our staff—with great ideas on how to best influence our players in a positive way and create better team unity and chemistry. Lou can be contacted at http://www.sportsleader.org.

Double Overtime

We finished this last chapter by presenting a challenge to men everywhere. I would like to invite you to visit my website at http://www.arealman.org. More copies of this book can be ordered from this site. This is a pretty neat website that presents several ideas on ways to promote the principles of being real men. Copies of my first book *"Beyond the Goal Line: The Quest for Victory in the Game of Life"* can also be purchased from this site. This website also lists ways that we can be better husbands and great fathers to our children, including a "tip of the month" feature that will present fun and creative ideas on how to better love and serve our families. Finally, this site contains some pretty awesome gift ideas, either for yourself or the most important men in your life. Check it out!

Gentlemen, it is time for us to step up. We have an opportunity to make a difference in the world around us by joining together for a common cause. Let us become real men—the kind of men that our wives, children, and God want us to be. May God bless each of us in these efforts!

www.arealman.org

Please visit my website to receive some great ideas on how to be a better husband, father, and role model in your community. This site also has some great gift ideas for those you love. More copies of this book can be ordered from this site. Please come visit us! God Bless!

www.arealman.org

CPSIA information can be obtained
at www.ICGtesting.com
Printed in the USA
BVOW11s2028030518
515184BV00002B/429/P